COOKING WITH FISH

COOKING WITH FISH
Rosamond Man

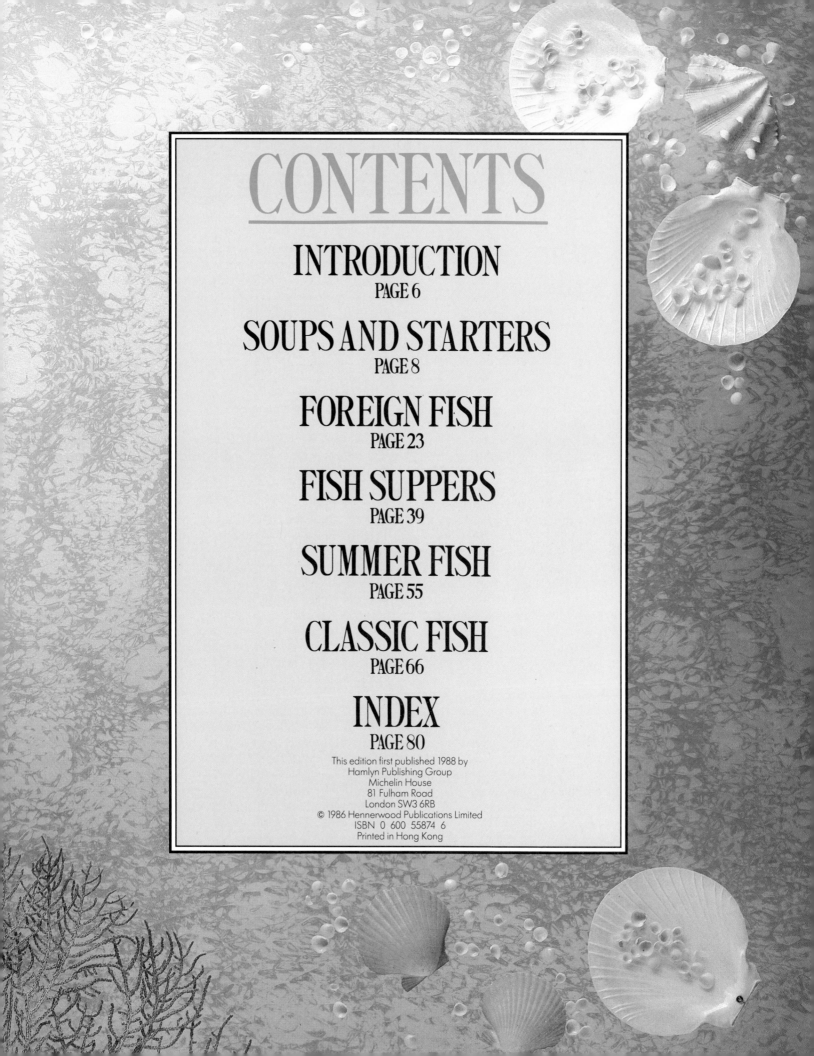

CONTENTS

INTRODUCTION
PAGE 6

SOUPS AND STARTERS
PAGE 8

FOREIGN FISH
PAGE 23

FISH SUPPERS
PAGE 39

SUMMER FISH
PAGE 55

CLASSIC FISH
PAGE 66

INDEX
PAGE 80

This edition first published 1988 by
Hamlyn Publishing Group
Michelin House
81 Fulham Road
London SW3 6RB
© 1986 Hennerwood Publications Limited
ISBN 0 600 55874 6
Printed in Hong Kong

INTRODUCTION

'Of all nacyons and countries England is beste served of Fysshe – not onely of al maner of see-fysshe but also of freshe water fysshe – an all maner of sorts of salte fysshe.' So said an English sixteenth-century writer in his 'Dyetary of Helth'.

Today, ever more health conscious, we are constantly urged to eat more of the fish which is so abundant in our waters. Yet we appear as reluctant as our forebears, who were compelled by law to eat fish on both Fridays and Saturdays – the penalty for non-observance being a hefty £3 fine, or three months' imprisonment!

It cannot be lack of choice, for there are fifty-two species of fish found around our islands, not including shellfish, freshwater fish or the smoked delicacies, for which we are justly famous. Even so, we are eating less fish than we did some twenty years ago, the average household consumption of fresh or frozen sea fish being only approximately 9.5 kilograms (21 pounds) each year. If one were to double, or even treble, that figure to allow for inland and cured fish consumption, it still amounts to a tiny dish, or fish, gracing our tables – just once a week. Furthermore, we are sadly unadventurous. For, of those fifty-two possible choices, we tend to ask for only three: cod, plaice and haddock, their sales far outstripping the much cheaper mackerel and herring, while the whiting (much more glamorous under its medieval name – the merling or marling, and rightly prized by the French) hardly figures at all.

The other delicious fish that swim around our shores we either ignore, or pass over because we are uncertain how to cook them. How many fishmongers regularly display John Dory, sea bream, grey and red mullet, turbot, halibut, shad, dabs, whitebait, pilchards, sprats, gurnard (often mistaken for red mullet – not so fine, but still delicious with its traditional flavouring of bacon), garfish (caught off the West Country, sold almost entirely to the East End of London), hake, squid, monkfish, or spider crabs? The last three in particular are hauled in by our Cornish fishermen, quickly packed in ice, and sent off to France!

In addition we have beautiful mussels – sweetly plump and orange in England, delicately tiny and pale apricot in Scotland; tiny brown shrimps – the best of all; Dublin Bay prawns or langoustine – the real scampi, alas hardly ever seen; lobsters – always expensive, but now available frozen in seawater at a much more realistic price; and, possibly most delicious of all, crabs – a still vastly underrated delicacy.

Perhaps it is modesty that has caused the decline of our great culinary traditions, particularly in the fish kitchen. But if we think, too, of the wonderful array of cured fish at our disposal and all the creatures quietly inhabiting our streams and rivers, maybe it is time to resuscitate our heritage. Not only is our smoked salmon the finest in the world but who else has Finnan haddocks; Arbroath smokies; Manx, Loch Fyne or Mallaig kippers; bloaters or smoked sprats?

Buying Fish

Despite this wealth of fish all around us, unless you actually live at the seaside, fish can be quite difficult to buy. The last decade has seen the rapid demise of the high street fishmonger and much frozen fish has already been breadcrumbed, sauced or otherwise embellished. But the scales are slowly turning. Nouvelle cuisine, holidays abroad, the rise in popularity of 'ethnic' restaurants and a greater concern about eating healthy food, have all combined to produce a renewed demand for the 'wet slab' fish shop. Look for a good variety on display, ideally with many of the fish still whole, then you can see the bright, convex eyes, firm, gleaming flesh and red gills, which all denote a beautifully fresh fish. The smell should be of the sea; lobsters and crabs should preferably be alive; Dublin Bay prawns raw, beheaded but still with their shells; and the service informative. You should be allowed to choose what you want; to pick up that lobster (it should be heavy for its size, and unmottled) or to feel gently behind the gills of the chosen fish (your finger should leave no mark, the flesh should be springy not spongy). The fishmonger should be able to tell you what to do with it, be willing to clean it (and show you how) and, above all, have trimmings available.

If possible, buy your fish whole and do the filleting yourself. It may demand a little more of your time, but you will then have the trimmings for stocks and soups and, most important, your fish will stay fresher, for it loses much of its succulence and taste once skinned and filleted. Many fish, particularly the larger ones, also benefit from being cooked whole, thus keeping all their moistness and taste intact, as well as their looks.

Cleaning and Cooking Fish

Even though the fishmonger will usually have cleaned the fish for you, it is as well to know the essentials. First, cut off all the fins (and spiny barbs), then, using a blunt, large-bladed knife, remove the scales under cold running water and working from tail to head. Next slit it open along the belly to remove the insides. Small fish can have the intestines removed through the gills – a chicken-boning knife is ideal for this. Rinse well, dry, then cut off the head and tail if you prefer and your fish is ready. Skinning and filleting vary slightly according to the fish but neither are complicated operations and details are given through the book with the appropriate recipes, as are methods for dealing with shellfish.

When it comes to cooking the fish, there are a multitude of choices: poaching, steaming, baking (en papillote or not), frying, grilling and barbecuing all produce delicious dishes. The only thing you should never do is throw your fish into fast and furious boiling water, for it will instantly lose all its flavour. Cooking times are generally not long, thus keeping the nutrients and taste of the fish intact and helping the hurried cook. Cold fish dishes, too, are a boon in this harried day and age, and much neglected in Britain, though popular in sunnier climes. Many are extremely delicious, allowing the flavours to develop more fully than in a hot dish.

Fish soups, too, are largely ignored in the British kitchen, yet again give us many delicious and versatile dishes, from hearty, warming chowders and thick soups – abundant in different varieties of fish and vegetables, to thin clear consommés – ideal for a summer dinner party. Many are dependent on fish stock, as are some of the classic sauces, and it is here that the trimmings come into their own. The stock is easily made, and always useful to have in the freezer.

Collect together from fish filleted at home or by your fishmonger, 1–1.5 kg (2–3 lb) fish trimmings. Include a selection of heads, tails, bones and skin, ideally with a salmon head and/or some sole and turbot bones among them – their gelatinous texture improving the stock enormously. Put them in a large pan with a sliced onion, carrot and leek. And a bouquet garni (made of parsley, chervil, thyme and bay leaf), a few peppercorns (no salt as the stock is later reduced), 2 teaspoons cider or white wine vinegar, and a little white wine if wished (or an extra tablespoon of vinegar plus a pinch of sugar). Cover with 1.75 litres (3 pints) cold water, bring to the boil, skim and simmer gently for 30 minutes. (Don't leave it for longer as the bones will release too much gelatine and the stock will taste of glue.) Strain, then boil to reduce by about a quarter. Cool and freeze, putting some of the stock in ice cube trays, so if only a spoonful or two is needed for a particular recipe, it is easily to hand. Pack the cubes in bags, once frozen.

Lobster and crab shells also make delicious stocks, useful as a base for soups and stews. Once the meat has been extracted, simply crush the shells and put into a pan (with the small claws if using a crab), add some grated lemon rind, a bay leaf, a few sprigs of parsley, a few peppercorns and 1.2 litres (2 pints) water. Simmer for about 30–40 minutes. Strain, then return to the pan and reduce by rapid boiling to about 600 ml (1 pint) before using or freezing. Prawn shells and heads can be used the same way, and both stocks can be frozen up to 2 months.

For baking fish, butter papers are a very useful item – they also help prevent an unappetizing skin forming on sauces needing to be kept warm. Keep the wrappers from blocks of butter, unscraped, in a box in the freezer, removing them 30 minutes before starting to cook the recipe.

In all areas of fish cooking, black and white pepper are frequently used and they are at their best when freshly ground. Indeed, this is true of all spices since they quickly lose their potency after grinding – and none so dramatically as allspice. If you have only one peppermill, simply tip out the black peppercorns, add a few allspice berries (or white peppercorns) and grind. The lingering flavour of the black pepper won't hurt at all, and any unground berries may be returned to their screw-top jar, the black peppercorns to their mill. But it really is worth investing in one or two extra mills, so that the spices can be easily ground as and when they are needed.

So, even if you can't get bream, or mullet, or monkfish, why not experiment with cod, or plaice or haddock? That nineteenth-century invention from Wapping – fish and chips – is, at its best, rightly one of England's national dishes. But there are a hundred other ways of cooking fish as well.

SOUPS AND STARTERS

HERRING-ROE STUFFED MUSHROOMS

The soft creaminess of herring roes combines well with the 'bite' and earthiness of the flat wild horse mushroom. If these are unavailable, button mushrooms can be used instead. Slice them finely and sauté for no more than 30 seconds, so that they are still crunchy, then mix into the herring paste and serve with Melba toast.

200 g (7 oz) unsalted butter
225 g (8 oz) herring roes
salt
freshly ground black pepper
about 2–3 tablespoons lemon juice
pinch of cayenne pepper or a few drops of Tabasco
¼ teaspoon dried dill
4 large flat or 8 medium mushrooms, stalks trimmed to
25 mm (1 inch)
2 tablespoons finely chopped fresh parsley
lemon wedges and sprigs of parsley, to serve (optional)

Preparation time: 5–10 minutes
Cooking time: 15–20 minutes

1. Melt 25 g (1 oz) butter in a large frying pan, add the roes and fry for 3–4 minutes, constantly turning until slightly firm all over.
2. Mash the roes with another 50 g (2 oz) butter, then season with salt, lots of pepper, the lemon juice, cayenne pepper or Tabasco and the dill.
3. Mix thoroughly, then taste, adding more lemon juice if necessary.
4. Melt the remaining butter in a small deep saucepan. Dip each mushroom quickly into the butter to coat completely.
5. Grill the mushrooms, flat side up, for 4–5 minutes, then turn over and grill for 2 minutes more.
6. Spread the roe paste over the flat side of each mushroom, then grill them under a medium heat for a further 3–5 minutes until the roe paste is golden brown and sizzling.
7. Sprinkle the mushrooms with the chopped parsley and then serve, with lemon wedges and sprigs of parsley if wished.

FRIED WHITEBAIT

Our nineteenth century forebears appreciated the virtues of these tiny fish, for the Thames estuary yielded abundant fresh supplies. Happily, nowadays most good fishmongers have plenty of whitebait in their freezers.

Serves 6
750 g (1½ lb) whitebait, thawed if frozen
150 ml (¼ pint) milk
8–10 tablespoons flour
salt
freshly ground white pepper
oil, for deep frying
To serve:
dill sprig, to garnish
cayenne pepper (optional)
lemon wedges
brown bread and butter

Preparation time: 10–15 minutes
Cooking time: 12–16 minutes

1. Coat the whitebait in the milk by putting them in batches, in a large sieve and pouring the milk over. Have a bowl underneath to catch the liquid, then you can return it to the jug and pour it over the next lot of fish.
2. Again working in batches, put 2 tablespoons of flour into a plastic bag, add some fish, and shake to coat well. Repeat, using more flour, until all the fish are floured.
3. Sprinkle with salt and pepper. Fill a deep fat fryer about two-thirds full with oil, with the basket in place, and heat to 190°C/375°F, or until a cube of bread turns golden in about 50 seconds.
4. Lift the basket out and put a quarter of the fish in it – any more will reduce the temperature of the oil and the fish will not be crisp. Fry for 3–4 minutes, then tip out into a large colander lined with paper towels. Let the oil reheat for 30 seconds, then cook the next batch of fish in the same way. Repeat until all the fish are cooked. To check, taste one, if it isn't really crunchy – fry them all again in batches for 1 minute per batch.
5. Drain well, garnish and serve immediately, sprinkled with cayenne pepper if used (the dish then becomes Devilled Whitebait), and accompanied by lemon wedges and thin brown bread and butter.

CRAB STICKS WITH SESAME SEED MAYONNAISE

2 large egg yolks
300 ml (½ pint) olive oil, at room temperature
¼ teaspoon sesame seed oil
freshly ground sea salt
freshly ground white pepper
pinch of cayenne pepper
1−2 teaspoons cider vinegar, to taste
2 tablespoons sesame seeds
24 crab sticks, thawed but chilled
crisp curly lettuce leaves and sprigs of dill, to garnish
(optional)

Preparation time: 5 minutes

Crab sticks with sesame seed mayonnaise; Herring-roe stuffed mushrooms

1. Make a basic mayonnaise with the egg yolks and oil as for Orange and Garlic Mayonnaise (page 10). Stir in the sesame seed oil and season with salt, white pepper and cayenne.
2. Whisk in 1 teaspoon vinegar, check the taste and add more if necessary. (This is a matter of taste, but traditionally mayonnaise should be gently tangy and not too sharp).
3. Put the sesame seeds in a frying pan. Either dry fry for a minute or so, constantly stirring, or put them under the grill for about 45 seconds until they turn golden. Watch them all the time for they catch very easily.
4. Stir the sesame seeds into the mayonnaise, then transfer to a serving bowl. Serve with the chilled crab sticks, garnished with lettuce leaves and dill sprigs.

9

BOURRIDE

*The essence of this classic Provençal dish is its
wonderfully garlicky sauce – aïoli. It's traditionally
made with 2 cloves per person, but if you're not used to
large quantities of garlic, start with a gentler amount.*

Serves 6–8
450 g (1 lb) fish trimmings (heads, bones, skin etc)
2 leeks, chopped
1 large onion, peeled and chopped
2–3 garlic cloves, peeled and halved
1 × 7.5 cm (3 inch) piece lemon or Seville orange peel
1 bay leaf
1 sprig fresh thyme
3–4 sprigs parsley
1 tablespoon wine vinegar
1 litre (1¾ pints) cold water
olive oil, for frying
450 g (1 lb) potatoes, finely sliced
1.5 kg (3 lb) whole fish fillets (monkfish, brill or John
Dory) thickly sliced
sea salt
freshly ground black pepper
6 slices white bread, crusts removed
4–5 tablespoons finely chopped fresh parsley, to garnish
For the aïoli:
4–8 garlic cloves, peeled
2 egg yolks, size 1
about 300 ml (½ pint) olive oil, preferably Provençal
white pepper
1–3 teaspoons lemon juice

*Preparation time: 20–30 minutes
Cooking time: 50 minutes–1 hour*

1. Rinse the fish trimmings under running water, removing any traces of blood. Put in a large pan with 1 leek, the onion, 1 garlic clove, if wished, the peel, herbs and vinegar. Add the water and simmer gently for 20–25 minutes.
2. Meanwhile, make the aïoli. Mash the garlic cloves with a good pinch of salt, then beat in the egg yolks.
3. Add a few drops of oil, whisking constantly, then a few more, still whisking, until the mixture is thick enough to absorb the oil in a thin, steady stream. This will take longer than when making ordinary mayonnaise, as the garlic 'thins' the eggs. When all the oil is added you should finish with a very thick, yellow mayonnaise. Season with white pepper and lemon juice to taste, then transfer to a small heavy-based pan and reserve.
4. Strain the cooked stock and discard the seasonings. Heat 1 tablespoon olive oil in a large pan, add the remaining leek and 1 garlic clove, and fry gently for 2–3 minutes, then arrange the potatoes in a layer on top, covering the base of the pan.
5. Lay the fish fillets on top of the potatoes, season lightly with salt and black pepper, then pour the strained stock over. Simmer gently for 10–20 minutes until the fish is just cooked and flakes easily – check after 10 minutes.
6. While the fish is simmering, pour enough oil into a large frying pan to cover the bottom. Rub both sides of the bread with the remaining clove of garlic, then fry, two at a time, until golden on both sides. Drain thoroughly on paper towels, cut into croûtons and put in a bowl.
7. Place the fish in the centre of a warmed dish and arrange the potatoes around it. Cover and keep warm.
8. Reduce the liquid left in the pan by fast boiling until you have a scant 450 ml (¾ pint). Check seasoning, then pour through a sieve on to the aïoli, stirring.
9. Put over a low heat and stir for 1–2 minutes until the sauce thickens slightly, then pour over the fish and potatoes. Garnish and serve with the croûtons.

GOUJONS OF SOLE WITH ORANGE
AND GARLIC MAYONNAISE

*Goujon is a French word, derived from the gudgeon, a
tiny fish, about 5–7.5 cm (2–3 inches) long. It refers to
the way the fillets are prepared for this dish.*

Serves 6
6 fillets Dover sole, about 750 g (1½–1¾ lb) total
weight
freshly ground sea salt
freshly ground black pepper
100 g (4 oz) unsalted butter
For the mayonnaise:
2 large egg yolks, at room temperature
300 ml (½ pint) olive or peanut oil, at room
temperature
2–3 garlic cloves, peeled and crushed
grated rind of ½ orange
1 tablespoon fresh orange juice
½–1 tablespoon lemon juice
freshly ground white pepper
To serve:
3 tablespoons finely chopped fresh parsley
orange slices

*Preparation time: 15 minutes
Cooking time: 7–8 minutes*

1. Cut each fillet into 3–4 long thin strips, then cut each strip into 7.5 cm (3 inch) long pieces. Sprinkle with salt and black pepper.
2. Make a basic mayonnaise by beating the egg yolks in a large bowl. Put the oil in a jug and add a few drops, beating all the time. Add a few more, gradually building up to a thin drizzle, beating constantly between additions so that the yolks absorb the oil smoothly. The finished mayonnaise should be very thick and glossy.

3. Flavour the mayonnaise by stirring in the garlic and orange rind, then whisk in the orange and lemon juice. Season lightly with salt and white pepper, then pour into a serving bowl.

4. Melt the butter in a large frying pan and when beginning to bubble add as many fish as the pan will hold in one layer. Fry quickly for about 1½ minutes each side until lightly golden, then remove with a slotted spoon. Quickly cook the rest.

5. Pile on to a warmed serving dish, sprinkle with the parsley, garnish with the orange slices and serve at once.

MINIATURE PRAWN KEBABS

450 g (1 lb) frozen prawns, cooked but unshelled
4 tablespoons olive oil
1 tablespoon lemon juice
1 teaspoon soy sauce
1 × 25 mm (1 inch) piece fresh root ginger, peeled and grated
¼ teaspoon cumin seeds, lightly ground
freshly ground sea salt
freshly ground black pepper
3 spring onions, green tops only, shredded diagonally
1 small bunch of fresh parsley, finely chopped
6 lemon wedges, to serve

Goujons of sole with orange and garlic mayonnaise; Miniature prawn kebabs

Preparation time: 30 minutes, plus marinating
Cooking time: 4–5 minutes

1. Shell the prawns, (keep the heads and shells to make soups or stock) and put into a deep dish.

2. Mix together the olive oil, lemon juice, soy sauce, ginger and cumin, then pour over the prawns. Stir to coat, cover and then leave to marinate for at least 1 hour (preferably unchilled as the flavours should be allowed to develop). Turn them once or twice during this time.

3. About 20 minutes before serving, put 12 bamboo skewers into water to soak – these are widely available from oriental food stores.

4. Sprinkle the prawns with a little salt and pepper, then thread them on to the soaked bamboo skewers – about 5 per skewer.

5. Cook under a hot grill for 4–5 minutes, turning the skewers halfway through and basting with a little of the marinade.

6. Make a bed of the shredded onion tops and chopped parsley on 6 small plates, and serve the skewers on top, with the lemon wedges. You could also supply a little jug of olive oil, for those who might like to sprinkle a few drops on their onion and parsley 'salad'.

SMOKED MACKEREL MOUSSE WITH MARINATED CUCUMBERS

Serves 6
For the mousse:
400 g (14 oz) smoked mackerel fillets
1 tablespoon powdered gelatine
3 tablespoons cold water
2–3 tablespoons lemon juice
3 tablespoons mayonnaise
3 tablespoons plain unsweetened yogurt
1–2 teaspoons creamed horseradish
¼ teaspoon ground ginger
cayenne pepper, to taste
freshly ground black pepper
2 large egg whites
For the marinated cucumbers:
1 medium cucumber
freshly ground sea salt
3 spring onions
1 tablespoon cider vinegar
½ teaspoon caster sugar
½ teaspoon dried mint
3 tablespoons finely chopped coriander or fresh parsley
sprigs of mint and cucumber slices, to garnish

Preparation time: 30 minutes, plus chilling
Cooking time: 3 minutes

1. Skin the mackerel fillets and remove any bones, then mash in a large bowl.
2. Sprinkle the gelatine over the water in a small bowl and stand in a pan of simmering water until dissolved. Take off the heat and cool slightly.
3. Add 2 tablespoons lemon juice to the mackerel together with the mayonnaise, yogurt, 1 teaspoon horseradish, the ginger, a pinch or two of cayenne pepper and a good grinding of black pepper. Quickly stir in the dissolved gelatine, beating thoroughly.
4. Whisk the egg whites until stiff peaks form, then fold into the mackerel mixture, gently but thoroughly.
5. Wet a 600 ml (1 pint) mould with cold water, then spoon in the mousse and chill for at least 3 hours.
6. One and a half hours before serving, halve the cucumber horizontally and remove the seeds. Cut the cucumber into strips, put on a plate and sprinkle generously with salt, then weight down with another plate. Leave for 30 minutes then rinse the salt off and dry.
7. Put the cucumber in a large bowl. Grate the bulbs of the spring onions into the bowl, then shred the green tops diagonally and add them too. Stir in the vinegar, sugar and mint and sprinkle with black pepper. Leave until ready to serve, stirring once or twice.
8. To serve, dip the bottom of the mould into very hot water for a few seconds, then put a plate over the top and quickly invert the mould on to the plate.
9. Mix the chopped coriander into the cucumber, then arrange around the mousse. Garnish and serve.

SCALLOPED SMOKED HADDOCK MOUSSELINES

Serves 6
450 g (1 lb) smoked haddock fillets
generous pinch of freshly grated nutmeg
¼ teaspoon paprika
pinch of ground cinnamon
freshly ground black pepper
3 large egg whites
300 ml (½ pint) fromage blanc
butter, for greasing
For the sauce:
100 g (4 oz) unsalted butter
150 ml (5 fl oz) double cream
1 × 25 mm (1 inch) piece fresh root ginger, peeled and grated
1–2 tablespoons lime juice
1–2 drops soy sauce
freshly ground sea salt
1 tablespoon finely chopped fresh parsley
lime slices, to garnish

Preparation time: 15 minutes
Cooking time: 15–25 minutes
Oven: 180°C, 350°F, Gas Mark 4

1. Skin the fish and remove as many bones as possible. Either work in a food processor until thoroughly mashed, or mince, then pound until reduced to a paste.
2. Season with nutmeg, paprika, cinnamon and a generous amount of pepper. Beat in the egg whites and when well blended add the fromage blanc and stir thoroughly. If you are using a food processor simply put all these ingredients into the bowl with the mashed fish and process for a minute or so until smooth.
3. Grease 6 large scallop shells, leaving a 25 mm (1 inch) edge ungreased, then spoon in the fish mixture, leaving the ungreased rims clear.
4. Make 6 bases of crumpled foil to support the shells then arrange the shells in a roasting pan. Pour in hot water to come just above the foil, under the shells. Cook the mousselines in the preheated oven for 15–25 minutes until just firm and set, then turn off the oven and leave the door ajar – the mousses will stay warm while you make the sauce, which is made at the last minute.
5. Melt the butter in a wide shallow pan over a low heat. When about to start bubbling, add the cream and raise the heat slightly. Stir in the ginger, lime juice and soy sauce, and season lightly with salt and pepper.
6. Stir the sauce for 3–4 minutes until it has thickened slightly, then add the parsley.
7. Transfer the scallop shells to serving plates (the weight of the mousse will keep them upright) and drizzle a little sauce over each one. Garnish and serve at once with the rest of the sauce in a jug.

PRAWN AND SPINACH TERRINE

Serves 6–8
750 g (1½ lb) fresh prawns, cooked but unshelled
2 large egg whites
¼ teaspoon juniper berries, crushed
1 teaspoon lemon juice
freshly ground sea salt
freshly ground black pepper
200 ml (7 fl oz) double cream
150 g (5 oz) fresh spinach
1 teaspoon butter, plus extra for greasing
pinch of freshly grated nutmeg
To garnish:
whole prawns
chives

Preparation time: 1 hour, plus chilling
Cooking time: 35–40 minutes
Oven: 160°C, 325°F, Gas Mark 3

1. Shell the prawns, (use the shells and heads for making stock). Put the prawns through a mincer, or purée in a food processor.
2. Add the egg whites, juniper berries, lemon juice, salt and pepper and mix in. Beat in the cream until smooth.
3. Select enough spinach leaves to line a 1 litre (1¾ pint) terrine. If the spinach is large-leafed, 5–7 should be enough, if the leaves are young and small you might need about 50 g (2 oz). Trim, wash and blanch the leaves in a large pan of boiling water for 45 seconds. Drain and rinse under cold water.
4. Grease the terrine well then line with the blanched spinach leaves – making sure they come right up to the top; don't worry if they overlap the edges a little.
5. Wash and trim the remaining spinach, shake off excess moisture, then chop finely. Melt the butter in a small pan, pile in the spinach and let it stew gently in the butter and its own juices for about 5 minutes until quite soft but not mushy. Season with nutmeg and a little salt and pepper.
6. Spread half the prawn mixture in the terrine, then arrange the spinach on top in a thin layer. Top with the remaining prawn mixture and smooth the top. Fold over any overlapping leaves.
7. Stand the terrine in a roasting pan half-filled with hot water and cook in the preheated oven for 30–35 minutes until the mousse is just set.
8. Take out of the oven and allow to cool. Chill for 4–5 hours.[F] Just before serving, turn the terrine on to a platter. Serve in slices, garnished.

[F] Can be frozen, although texture not as good. Freeze for 2–3 weeks only. Thaw overnight in the refrigerator.

LEFT TO RIGHT: *Smoked mackerel mousse with marinated cucumbers; Scalloped smoked haddock mousselines; Prawn and spinach terrine*

CLASSIC CLAM CHOWDER

Most fishmongers selling live clams will have washed them first but if they look sandy, give them a good scrub, discarding any that do not shut tightly when sharply tapped.

Serves 6–8
48–60 fresh clams, or frozen clams in their shells
40 g (1½ oz) butter
100 g (4 oz) salt pork belly or smoked streaky bacon, rinds removed, diced
2 large onions, peeled and finely chopped
2 celery stalks, diced
1–2 leeks, trimmed and cut into rings
2 tablespoons finely chopped fresh parsley
2 bay leaves
leaves from 1 sprig fresh thyme or ¼ teaspoon dried thyme
900 ml (1½ pints) cold water
ground nutmeg
freshly ground black pepper
finely ground sea salt (optional)
4–5 medium potatoes, diced
2 tablespoons flour
1–2 teaspoons Worcestershire sauce

Preparation time: 15–45 minutes (plus thawing if using frozen clams)
Cooking time: 35–40 minutes

1. Either open the clams as you would oysters, or put them on a baking sheet in the oven at 200°C, 400°F, Gas Mark 6 for 2–3 minutes until they open slightly, then remove and prise the shells apart. Frozen clams should be put in a bowl with warm water barely covering them for 30 minutes–1 hour. As soon as the shells start to open, prise them apart. In both instances, open the shells over a bowl to catch all the clam juice. Snip off the inedible black-tipped neck (it looks rather like a little tube) from each one. Roughly chop the coral-coloured and pinky flesh and leave the softer body meat whole.
2. Melt 25 g (1 oz) of the butter in a large pan. Add the pork or bacon and cook for about 5 minutes until the fat starts to run, then add the onions, cover and cook gently for 10 minutes.
3. Add the celery, leeks, parsley, bay leaves and thyme and cook for a further 5 minutes.
4. Add the reserved clam juice, the water and generous pinches of nutmeg and black pepper. Stir well then taste and add salt if necessary.
5. Add the potatoes and bring to the boil. Simmer gently for about 10 minutes until the potatoes are almost tender.
6. Meanwhile, mash the flour with the remaining butter until you have a smooth paste. Reserve.
7. Add the clams to the pan and simmer very gently for 3–4 minutes. The liquid must not boil or the clams will be tough and rubbery.

8. Add a piece of butter and flour mixture (beurre manié) to the pan, stirring well. When dissolved stir in a little more, and continue until all has been added. Stir for another 3–4 minutes until the soup thickens slightly.
9. Increase the heat under the chowder for 10 seconds, then remove from the stove. Add the Worcestershire sauce. Stir quickly and serve immediately.

PRAWN BISQUE

Serves 6
1 kg (2 lb) prawns, cooked but unpeeled, thawed if frozen
75 g (3 oz) butter
1 onion, peeled and finely chopped
1 large carrot, finely chopped
1 celery stalk, finely chopped
3 tablespoons gin or brandy
150 ml (5 fl oz) dry sherry or white wine
2 sprigs parsley
1 sprig fresh thyme
1 bay leaf
3 tablespoons long-grain rice
1.2 litres (2 pints) cold water
freshly ground sea salt
freshly ground white pepper
cayenne pepper, to taste
generous pinch of ground nutmeg
175 ml (6 fl oz) double cream
finely chopped fresh parsley, to garnish

Preparation time: 30 minutes
Cooking time: 45 minutes

1. Peel the prawns, reserving the heads and shells.
2. Melt 25 g (1 oz) butter in a large deep pan. Add the vegetables and fry gently for 10 minutes. Add the prawn shells. Heat the gin in a ladle, over a burner, then pour into the pan and, standing well back, immediately set light to it. Shake the pan until the flames die down.
3. Add the sherry, herbs and rice, then pour in the water. Quickly bring to the boil, then reduce the heat and simmer for 30 minutes.
4. Blend in a liquidizer, then sieve to remove any remaining shell and make the soup really smooth.
5. Reserve about 18 prawns, then blend the rest with some of the strained stock to give a thick purée. Thin down with a little more stock then return to the rinsed-out pan. Gradually stir in the rest of the stock and season with salt, pepper, a touch of cayenne and a pinch of nutmeg.
6. Whisk in the remaining butter, a little at a time, then stir in all but 4 tablespoons of the cream, and the reserved prawns. Bring to boiling point, then pour into a warm soup tureen. Drizzle the rest of the cream over, sprinkle with parsley and serve.

MUSSEL CHOWDER

Serves 4–6

1.5 kg (3 lb) or 3 pints fresh mussels
1 large onion, peeled and finely chopped
6 tablespoons finely chopped fresh parsley
2–3 garlic cloves, peeled and finely chopped
1 mace blade, crumbled
1 bay leaf
300 ml (½ pint) dry white wine
900 ml (1½ pints) milk
2–3 strands saffron
½ teaspoon ground cinnamon
pinch of ground allspice
finely ground sea salt
freshly ground white pepper
400 g (14 oz) canned or frozen sweetcorn kernels
1 tablespoon flour
1 tablespoon butter
4–6 tablespoons soured cream
4 tablespoons snipped fresh chives

Preparation time: 25–30 minutes
Cooking time: 35–40 minutes

1. Scrub the mussels under cold running water with a clean hard brush, scraping off any barnacles and tugging off any beards. *Discard any broken mussels and any that do not shut when given a sharp tap*. Cover with cold water and leave while preparing the stock.

2. Put the onion, parsley, garlic, mace and bay leaf in a large pan with the white wine and simmer for 5–6 minutes.

3. Add half the mussels (unless your pan is large and wide) and cover tightly. Steam for 4–5 minutes over a high heat until the mussels have opened, then transfer to a large colander, *discarding any that have not opened*. Cook the remaining mussels the same way. Reserve 18–20 whole mussels and shell the rest. Put all the mussels in the colander and cover them.

4. Add the milk to the pan. Put the saffron in a cup, pour a couple of tablespoons of boiling water over and stir until the colour starts to run. Add to the pan together with the cinnamon, allspice, salt and a generous pinch of white pepper. Bring to the boil then add the sweetcorn and simmer for 10 minutes.

5. Mash the flour and butter together to make a smooth paste (beurre manié). Take a small piece and add to the pan, stir until dissolved then gradually add the rest, stirring after each addition. Simmer for 5–6 minutes to 'cook' the beurre manié but don't let it boil, or the flour will leave an after taste.

6. Check the seasoning, adding a little more salt or pepper if necessary, then add all the mussels, keeping the unshelled ones near the top. Reheat gently for 2–3 minutes, then lightly stir in the soured cream. Sprinkle the chives over and serve at once.

LEFT TO RIGHT: *Classic clam chowder; Prawn bisque; Mussel chowder*

SMOKED HADDOCK AND FENNEL
SOUP

Serves 6
750 g (1½ lb) smoked haddock
1.2 litres (2 pints) milk
2 tablespoons olive oil
1 fennel bulb, finely chopped, leaves reserved and finely chopped
finely ground sea salt
freshly ground white pepper
freshly ground black pepper
150 ml (¼ pint) crème fraîche
1 tablespoon dry sherry
2–3 drops Worcestershire sauce
pinch of paprika or cayenne pepper, to garnish

Preparation time: 5–10 minutes
Cooking time: 30 minutes

1. To remove excess salt, rinse the haddock in cold water then put in a pan and cover with boiling water. Leave for 5 minutes, then drain and rinse again.
2. Return haddock to the pan, cover with the milk and bring to the boil. Cover and simmer for 15–20 minutes.
3. Meanwhile, heat the oil, add the fennel bulb and cook over a high heat for 1–2 minutes. Reduce the heat and cook gently for 10 minutes until opaque.
4. Transfer the haddock to a plate and allow to cool slightly. Strain the milk, then pour into a liquidizer.
5. Discard the skin and bones from the haddock. Flake the flesh lightly and add to the liquidizer together with the fennel. Purée and return to the rinsed-out pan.
6. Taste and add a little salt if necessary, then season with white and black pepper and stir in all but 3 tablespoons of the crème fraîche. Heat to just below boiling point, then add the sherry and Worcestershire sauce.
7. Pour into bowls and put a spoonful of the reserved crème fraîche on top. Garnish with a sprinkling of paprika or cayenne and the chopped fennel leaves.

HOT AND SOUR FISH SOUP

Serves 4–6
750 g (1½ lb) fish trimmings, (bones, skin, etc.,
including some sole trimmings, if possible)
2 large onions, peeled
2 cloves
2 bay leaves
3 parsley sprigs
1 mace blade, crumbled
6 white peppercorns, plus ¼ teaspoon freshly ground
white pepper
1.75 litres (3 pints) cold water
1 tablespoon oil
2 garlic cloves, peeled and chopped
½ teaspoon dried marjoram
¼ teaspoon turmeric
generous pinch of ground nutmeg
1 teaspoon sugar
3–4 tablespoons cider vinegar
2 tablespoons soy sauce
1 kg (2 lb) haddock, cod or any other firm white fish
(or a mixture of several types)
100 g (4 oz) peeled prawns
3 tablespoons finely chopped fresh parsley or coriander
leaves
1 bunch spring onions, bulbs sliced and green tops
shredded diagonally

Preparation time: 20–25 minutes
Cooking time: 1¼ hours

1. Rinse the fish trimmings under cold running water, removing any traces of blood, then put into a large pan with one onion, studded with the cloves, the bay leaves, parsley, mace and peppercorns. Cover with the water and bring slowly to the boil. Skim, then simmer gently for 25 minutes.
2. Strain, discarding the fish trimmings and all the seasonings. Return the stock to the rinsed-out pan and boil hard until it is reduced to just 1.2 litres (2 pints).
3. Heat the oil in another pan, finely chop the second onion, and add to the pan, and cook very gently for 10 minutes. Add the garlic, marjoram, turmeric, nutmeg and ¼ teaspoon white pepper. Stir for 1–2 minutes, then add the reduced stock. Bring to the boil, stir in the sugar, together with the cider vinegar and soy sauce, then simmer for 10 minutes.
4. Meanwhile, skin the fish and cut into cubes or long, thin strips, carefully removing as many large bones as possible.
5. Add the fish to the pan and cook for 5–6 minutes only, no longer or the fish will disintegrate. Taste and add more pepper if necessary – the soup should have quite a 'bite' without being searingly hot.

LEFT TO RIGHT: *Hot and sour fish soup; Crab and spinach chowder*

6. Stir in the peeled prawns and heat through gently for 3–4 minutes. Stir in the chopped parsley or coriander and sliced and shredded pieces of spring onions and pour the soup into individual bowls.

CRAB AND SPINACH CHOWDER

Serves 6
50 g (2 oz) butter
1 large onion, peeled and finely chopped
100 g (4 oz) salt pork belly or smoked streaky bacon,
cut into large dice
450 g (1 lb) fresh spinach, trimmed, washed and finely
chopped or 225 g (8 oz) frozen leaf spinach
300 ml (½ pint) crab or prawn stock or water
600 ml (1 pint) milk
1 bay leaf
2–3 sprigs parsley
5 medium potatoes, finely chopped
finely ground sea salt
freshly ground black pepper
½ teaspoon ground cinnamon
1 mace blade, crumbled
½–1 teaspoon curry powder, to taste
400 g (14 oz) canned white crabmeat, drained, or
1 large fresh cooked crab
175 ml (6 fl oz) double cream
1 tablespoon lemon juice

Preparation time: 15 minutes (1 hour if using fresh crab)
Cooking time: 45 minutes

1. Melt the butter in a large saucepan, add the onion, cover and cook gently for 10 minutes. Add the pork or bacon and cook for 5 minutes.
2. Add the spinach and allow to stew for 10 minutes, then pour in the shellfish stock or water and the milk. Add the bay leaf and parsley and bring to the boil.
3. Stir in the potatoes. If using salt pork taste for saltiness before seasoning with salt and pepper. Add the cinnamon, mace blade and curry powder to taste. Simmer gently for about 10 minutes until the potatoes are almost tender.
4. Add the crabmeat (if using fresh crab, see page 59) and the cream and gently bring to the boil. Stir in the lemon juice, allow to bubble for 1–2 minutes, then serve at once.

Crème fraîche is a French product, now widely available. It consists of cream that has been allowed to ferment slightly and thicken. Tangy without being sour, it is less rich than double cream, and adds a hint of sharpness. If unobtainable, mix 2 parts double cream with 1 part soured cream or use cream seasoned with a little lemon juice.

SHRIMP BUTTER

Potted shrimps are a well known English speciality. Less famous (undeservedly) is this Scottish dish – a beautiful pale yellow cream flecked pink with prawns.

Serves 6
350 g (12 oz) fresh prawns, cooked but unshelled
600 ml (1 pint) water
225 g (8 oz) smoked haddock
2–3 anchovy fillets, chopped
¼ teaspoon ground cinnamon
pinch of freshly ground allspice
pinch of paprika
1–2 teaspoons lemon juice
freshly ground black pepper
1 teaspoon Kirsch
175 g (6 oz) unsalted butter, softened
To garnish:
tarragon leaves
dill sprigs

Preparation time: 30–35 minutes, plus chilling
Cooking time: 45 minutes

1. Shell the prawns, putting the shells and heads into a large pan. Add the water, bring to the boil and simmer for about 20–25 minutes. Chop the prawns quite finely and set aside.
2. Strain the stock, discarding the shells, and return to the pan together with the haddock. Simmer for 10–15 minutes until the fish flakes easily, then remove from the pan (reserving the stock) and leave to cool slightly.
3. When cool enough to handle, skin the haddock and remove as many bones as possible. Put in a large bowl with a couple of tablespoons of the stock (use the rest for soup) and mash well. Add the anchovy fillets and beat in well, then add the spices, 1 teaspoon lemon juice and a generous grinding of black pepper. Stir in the Kirsch.
4. Little by little, beat in half the butter, then fold in the chopped prawns, beating well to distribute the prawns evenly and give a really smooth cream.
5. Adjust the seasoning, adding more lemon juice if necessary (the haddock will probably provide enough salt) then pack into a small soufflé dish – traditionally the butter is always served in a white china dish. Smooth the top.
6. Melt the remaining butter in a small pan. When it is just about to froth, pour through a muslin-lined or very fine sieve on to the paste (making sure no sediment goes through). Chill for at least 2 hours.[A][F]
7. Garnish and serve with Melba toast.

[A] Once covered with clarified butter the paste can be chilled for up to 48 hours.
[F] Cover and freeze for up to 4 weeks. Thaw overnight in refrigerator.

SMOKED SALMON MILLE-FEUILLE

Serves 8–10
225 g (8 oz) frozen puff pastry, thawed
flour, for dusting
1 egg, beaten
225 g (8 oz) smoked salmon, coarsely minced
100 g (4 oz) cream cheese
50 g (2 oz) Feta cheese, crumbled
3 tablespoons plain unsweetened yogurt
pinch of freshly ground allspice
¼ teaspoon paprika
freshly ground white pepper
tarragon leaves and cherry tomatoes, to garnish

Preparation time: 30 minutes, plus chilling (optional)
Cooking time: 20 minutes
Oven: 220°C, 425°F, Gas Mark 7; then 190°C, 375°F, Gas Mark 5 (for reheating)

1. Roll out the pastry on a lightly floured board, being careful not to break it, into a 19 cm (7½ inch) square. Cut to a 19 cm (7½ inch) diameter circle, then very lightly score 8–10 'wedges' on the top.
2. Brush a baking sheet with cold water, put the pastry on it and glaze with the beaten egg, taking care not to let any run down over the cut edges of the pastry. Bake in the preheated oven for 15 minutes until puffed and golden.
3. Cool slightly, then split in half horizontally, and allow to cool completely. [F]
4. Meanwhile, mix the smoked salmon, cream and Feta cheeses with the yogurt, then add the allspice, paprika, and pepper to taste. Beat well together. [F]
5. When the pastry is quite cold, spread the filling over the bottom layer and put on the top. Cover with cling film and chill until ready to serve. [A]
6. To serve, reheat the oven, cover the cake with foil to prevent overbrowning and bake for 5 minutes. Garnish with tarragon and cherry tomatoes.

[A] The cake can be prepared the previous day, then covered with cling film and chilled overnight.
[F] Freeze pastry and filling separately for up to 6 weeks, wrapped in foil. Thaw overnight in refrigerator and assemble just before ready to eat.
[M] To thaw pastry in the microwave, put half of it on a paper towel and cover with the remaining sheet. Heat on Defrost for 3–5 minutes, turning halfway through, repeat with the remaining half. Stand for 15 minutes before using. To thaw the filling, turn into a suitable bowl and heat on Defrost for 8–12 minutes, stirring and breaking up gently as required. Stand for 20 minutes before using.

Shrimp butter; Smoked salmon mille-feuille

DEVILLED SARDINE PASTE

Canned sardines are curious creatures in that, like fine wines, they mature with age. There even used to be a club in London that met once a year to discuss the current 'vintage' and sample others from the 'cellar'. So keep a good stock and turn the cans over occasionally so the oil can blend with the fish. Always buy a good brand, preferably in olive oil, although some of the finest Portuguese sardines are now canned in other vegetable oil.

Serves 6
3 × 120 g (4½ oz) cans sardines, drained
up to 275 g (10 oz) unsalted butter, slightly softened
3–4 tablespoons lemon juice
freshly ground sea salt or Maldon salt
freshly ground black pepper
cayenne pepper, to taste
<u>To serve:</u>
lemon wedges
Melba toast
Preparation time: 5–15 minutes, plus chilling

1. Mash the sardines and 75 g (3 oz) butter to a smooth purée in a food processor or with a fork.
2. Add 3 tablespoons lemon juice, salt and pepper and purée again. Taste and add more butter if necessary; the texture must not be too dry. Adjust the seasoning if necessary, then beat in cayenne pepper to taste; the paste should be fairly spicy.
3. Pack into small ramekins, smooth the tops and chill for at least 45 minutes.[A][F]
4. Serve the sardine paste, chilled, with lemon wedges and Melba toast.

[A] The pots of paste can be prepared 3–4 days in advance, but should be covered with clarified butter before storing. Melt 100 g (4 oz) unsalted butter in a small saucepan. When completely melted and just starting to froth (do not let it bubble), pour through a muslin-lined or very fine sieve into a bowl making sure no sediment goes through. Spoon over the ramekins, allow to cool and chill until required. If preparing in advance, use 275 g (10 oz) butter in the paste, or it will dry out.
[F] Cover and freeze for 3–4 weeks. Thaw overnight in refrigerator.

TUNA CREAMS ON CHINESE LEAVES

Serves 6–8
350 g (12 oz) canned tuna fish, drained
1 medium onion, peeled and grated or minced
225 g (8 oz) Chinese leaves, very finely chopped
caster sugar, to taste
1 tablespoon cider vinegar
3–4 tablespoons mayonnaise
1 tablespoon fromage blanc or plain unsweetened
yogurt
½ teaspoon Dijon mustard
oil, for frying
2 large slices white bread, crusts removed
finely ground sea salt or Maldon salt
freshly ground black pepper
To serve:
6–8 whole Chinese leaves
2 tablespoons finely chopped fresh chervil or parsley

Preparation time: 20 minutes
Cooking time: 4–5 minutes

1. Flake the tuna, then mash with the onion.
2. Sprinkle the chopped Chinese leaves with a large pinch of sugar and the vinegar and stir to mix.
3. Combine 3 tablespoons mayonnaise with the fromage blanc or yogurt and mustard, then mix into the chopped Chinese leaves. Add the tuna and fold in thoroughly.
4. Pour enough oil into a large frying pan to cover the bottom. Heat until nearly smoking, then add the bread (one slice at a time if necessary). Cook both sides for 2–3 minutes until golden on both sides. Drain well, then cut into croûtons.
5. Taste the tuna mixture; if it seems a little dry add the remaining mayonnaise. Season with salt and black pepper.[A]
6. Arrange one whole Chinese leaf on each plate and spoon the tuna cream on top.
7. Just before serving, sprinkle each plate with croûtons and chopped chervil or parsley.

[A] The tuna cream mixture can be prepared 24 hours in advance, then covered with cling film and kept chilled. Bring to room temperature before serving.

TWO SALMON TERRINE

Elegant and economical, this terrine not only stretches a little smoked salmon a long way, but it transforms its canned cousin. If you can buy a small tailpiece of fresh salmon – even better. Wrap it in generously buttered foil and bake at 180°C, 350°F, Gas Mark 4, for 20–30 minutes until it flakes easily.

Serves 6
175 g (6 oz) smoked salmon, finely sliced
350 g (12 oz) canned red salmon, drained
¼ teaspoon dried dill
2 teaspoons creamed horseradish
2–3 tablespoons fresh lime juice
1 teaspoon paprika
large pinch of ground allspice
finely ground sea salt
freshly ground white pepper
Tabasco, to taste
6 tablespoons crème fraîche (see page 17)
3 tablespoons cold water
1½ tablespoons powdered gelatine
2 egg whites, size 1
black lumpfish roe and chervil, to garnish
To serve:
freshly ground black pepper
lime wedges
Melba toast

*Preparation time: 20–25 minutes, plus chilling
Cooking time: 5 minutes*

1. Rinse a 600 ml (1 pint) terrine or loaf tin with cold water. Either line the base only with non-stick silicone paper or line the whole tin with cling film. Use the smoked salmon to line the tin completely, slightly overlapping it; don't worry if a little salmon overlaps edges of the tin.
2. Mash the canned salmon in a large bowl and add the dill, horseradish, 2 tablespoons lime juice, the paprika, allspice, a little salt, white pepper and Tabasco to taste. Mix thoroughly. Stir in the crème fraîche then taste, adding the last tablespoon of lime juice if necessary.
3. Put the water in a small basin, sprinkle the gelatine on top, then stand in a pan of simmering water until the gelatine has dissolved. Allow to cool slightly, then stir into the fish mixture.
4. Whisk the egg whites until they hold soft peaks, then fold into the mixture lightly but thoroughly. Turn into the lined mould, then fold any overlapping strips of salmon over the mixture. Chill for at least 3 hours.
5. Unmould just before serving. Garnish, sprinkle with black pepper and serve with lime wedges, Melba toast and extra Tabasco, for those who like it.

Tuna creams on Chinese leaves; Two salmon terrine

MUSSELS A LA CREME

Mussels must be one of the most under-rated shellfish in the British Isles. They are nutritious, cheap, and, with their dark blue shells and bright orange-pink flesh, highly decorative. Many people are daunted by their preparation, but that's only a question of time, and nowadays you can buy ready cleaned mussels which simply need rinsing and the beards pulling off.

Serves 6–8
2.25 kg (5 lb) or 5 pints mussels
1 large onion, peeled and very finely chopped
2–3 garlic cloves, peeled and finely chopped
6 tablespoons finely chopped fresh parsley
300 ml (½ pint) dry white wine
300 ml (½ pint) double cream
freshly ground sea salt
freshly ground black pepper
1–2 tablespoons lemon juice

*Preparation time: 45 minutes–1 hour
Cooking time: 15 minutes*

1. Fill the sink with cold water, tip in the mussels and swirl around. If the water becomes very sandy or cloudy, drain the sink and repeat the process until the water remains clear.
2. Scrape the mussels, removing any barnacles with a solid knife (an oyster knife is ideal).
3. Scrub all the shells with a clean hard brush, tug away beards protruding from the shells – they will come away easily if you pull hard and quickly. *Discard any broken mussels and any that do not close quickly when given a sharp tap.* Discard any which seem unduly heavy for their size. They are probably full of mud and will spoil the final dish. Rinse once again under cold running water.
4. Put the onion, garlic and half the parsley into a very large pan with the wine. Bring quickly to the boil, then simmer for about 5 minutes.
5. Add the mussels, in batches if you do not have a large enough pan, cover tightly and leave for 4–5 minutes over a high heat. All the mussels should have opened by then unless the pan is too crowded, in which case remove the open ones on the bottom and steam the rest for about 30 seconds more.
6. As they are cooked, put the mussels in a large serving bowl, *discarding any that have not opened.* Once all the mussels are cooked, strain the liquor left in the pan to remove any traces of sand, return it to the rinsed-out pan and add the cream.
7. Bring rapidly to the boil, add salt, pepper and lemon juice to taste and allow to bubble for 1–2 minutes until very slightly thickened. Pour over the mussels and serve at once with the rest of the parsley sprinkled on top. Serve in large soup bowls with lots of crusty bread to mop up the delicious sauce.

FOREIGN FISH

PRAWN AND SPINACH PILAU

Serves 6
750 g (1 lb) cooked prawns in their shells
1 × 5 cm (2 inch) piece lemon peel
3 parsley sprigs
1 thyme sprig
1 bay leaf
6 white peppercorns, lightly crushed
1.2 litres (2 pints) water
750 g (1½ lb) fresh spinach, or 400 g (14 oz) frozen leaf
spinach, thawed
350 g (12 oz) long-grain rice
4 tablespoons olive oil
2 large onions, peeled and finely chopped
1 garlic clove, peeled and crushed
freshly grated nutmeg
Maldon or sea salt
freshly ground white pepper

Preparation time: 35–40 minutes
Cooking time: about 50 minutes

1. Shell the prawns and put the heads and shells into a large pan with the lemon peel, herbs and peppercorns. Add the cold water and bring to the boil, then simmer for 20 minutes. Strain and reserve the stock.[A]
2. Wash fresh spinach then chop off and discard tough stalks. Shred finely. Thawed frozen spinach only needs to be squeezed to extract moisture, then chopped.
3. Measure and note the volume of rice, rinse in boiling water and soak in fresh boiled water for 5 minutes.
4. Heat the oil in a large saucepan, add the onions and cook gently for about 5 minutes, until starting to soften. Add the garlic and spinach and stir-fry for 2–3 minutes.
5. Drain the rice and add to the pan, stirring until it gleams with a light coating of oil, then grate over a generous amount of nutmeg. Measure out the same volume of prawn stock as the rice and pour over the rice. Season well, bring quickly to the boil, bubble for 10 seconds, then reduce the heat, add the prawns, cover and cook for 15–20 minutes until the liquid is absorbed.
6. Turn off the heat, stir the pan then cover and leave for 5 minutes to 'fluff' the rice. Serve immediately.

[A] The stock may be prepared up to 6 hours in advance. Keep the prawns chilled and covered.

COD SOFRITO

Sofrito is a Spanish word, adopted by the Sephardic Jews, to cover the cooking technique whereby fish, meat or poultry is gently poached in a mixture of oil, lemon juice and a little water, usually spiced with turmeric to colour it a delicate primrose yellow. The dish may be eaten hot or, even more delicious, left until cold – when the liquid lightly sets to give a delicately flavoured jelly.

Serves 6
1 kg (2 lb) cod fillet, skinned
4 tablespoons olive or corn oil
1 large onion, peeled and finely sliced
1 garlic clove, peeled and crushed
about 300 ml (½ pint) fish stock (page 7)
3–4 tablespoons lemon juice
½ teaspoon turmeric
1 × 5 cm (2 inch) piece cinnamon stick
Maldon or sea salt
freshly ground white pepper
finely chopped fresh parsley, to garnish

Preparation time: 10 minutes, plus cooling if wished
Cooking time: 25–30 minutes (excluding the fish stock)

1. Rinse the cod fillet, then cut evenly into thin slices or cubes.
2. Heat the oil in a large pan, add the onion and cook gently for 10 minutes until softened. Add the garlic and fry gently for another 5 minutes.
3. Add 150 ml (¼ pint) of the fish stock, 3 tablespoons of the lemon juice and the turmeric. Bring just to the boil. Add the fish, in one layer if possible, otherwise pack it tightly into the pan, burying the cinnamon stick in the middle. Sprinkle with salt and pepper, then simmer gently for 10–15 minutes, adding 2 tablespoons fish stock every 2–3 minutes and turning the fish once if it is in more than one layer.
4. When the fish is just done, taste the stock, adding a tablespoon more lemon juice if necessary, then pile on to a serving dish and sprinkle with lots of chopped parsley. Either serve immediately or, if you wish, leave to cool to room temperature.

TOP TO BOTTOM: *Cod sofrito; Prawn and spinach pilau*

SCALLOPS PROVENCALE

Scallops are one of the finest shellfish, sadly with a price to match, but well worth the extravagance for a special event. Buy them fresh from the fishmonger, who will usually display them open on the smaller, flat shell. Ask if you can have the deeper curved shell as well, to serve the scallops on. If you should buy them unopened, simply put under a very hot grill for 1–1½ minutes until the shells start to open up, then it's an easy matter to prise them apart. Be sure that you don't leave them for longer than that or they will start to cook and will be tough and rubbery for the recipe.

Serves 4–6
12 large scallops
Maldon or sea salt
freshly ground black pepper
3–4 tablespoons lemon juice
100–150 g (4–5 oz) unsalted butter
1 tablespoon olive oil
6 tablespoons home-made dried breadcrumbs
2–3 garlic cloves, peeled and finely chopped
4 tablespoons finely chopped fresh parsley
lemon wedges, to serve, optional

*Preparation time: 15–20 minutes
Cooking time: 5 minutes*

1. Detach the scallops from the shells, separating the coral from the white flesh. Cut off and discard any black pieces and the greyish gristle around the white flesh, then cut each scallop in half to give 2 flat discs. Scrub and thoroughly dry the deep curved shells if you have been able to get them.
2. Put the discs into a shallow bowl, sprinkle them lightly with salt and black pepper, then pour over the lemon juice.
3. Melt 50 g (2 oz) butter in a large frying pan, add the oil, then the breadcrumbs and gently fry for 2–3 minutes until lightly crisp. Add another 25 g (1 oz) butter if necessary – the breadcrumbs shouldn't burn but neither should they become too greasy. When they are golden and crisp, tip the breadcrumbs into a bowl and reserve.
4. Wipe the pan clean with paper towels and return to the heat. Melt the remaining 50 g (2 oz) butter and when just starting to bubble, add the scallop discs and fry for 1–2 minutes. Stir in the finely chopped garlic and parsley, then add the corals and continue cooking for another minute.
5. Mix in the breadcrumbs, then quickly divide between the shells or small serving dishes and serve immediately with lemon wedges if wished.

Scallops provençale; Sole fillets with soy and ginger

SOLE FILLETS WITH SOY AND GINGER

Serves 6
500–750 g (1¼–1½ lbs) sole fillets, skinned
2 egg whites
1 teaspoon cornflour
½ teaspoon Maldon or sea salt
3 tablespoons peanut or grapeseed oil
1 × 5 cm (2 inch) piece fresh root ginger, peeled and grated
1 large garlic clove, peeled and very finely chopped
3 tablespoons soy sauce
1 tablespoon dry sherry
3 tablespoons fish stock (page 7)
3 spring onions, cut into matchstick strips

*Preparation time: 15 minutes, plus marinating
Cooking time: 6 minutes*

1. Cut the sole into long thin strips. Beat the egg whites, cornflour and salt until frothy, then pour over the fish, mixing well. Chill for 20 minutes.
2. Heat the oil in a wok or large frying pan. When nearly smoking, add the fish and stir-fry over a fairly high heat for 2 minutes. Remove from the pan with a slotted spoon, then discard all but 1 tablespoon of the oil.
3. Add the ginger and chopped garlic and stir-fry for 1 minute, then pour in the soy sauce, sherry and fish stock. Bring to the boil quickly, then bubble for 2 minutes.
4. Return the fish to the pan and heat through for 1 minute, stirring constantly, then pile on to a warmed serving dish, sprinkling with the spring onion tops and serve at once, with boiled rice or baby corn-cobs.

GRILLED SARDINES WITH OREGANO

A classic eastern Mediterranean dish. Frozen sardines are widely available and will keep well in the freezer up to 6 weeks. Thaw in the refrigerator overnight, then clean by slipping a thin-pointed knife through the gills and nicking out the innards. For a fuller flavour and an authentic Mediterranean touch, leave them whole.

Serves 4–6
1.5 kg (3 lb) large sardines, thawed if frozen
Maldon or sea salt
freshly ground black and white pepper
100 ml (3½ fl oz) olive oil
3–4 tablespoons lemon juice
1 tablespoon dried oregano
1 garlic clove, peeled and crushed
To serve:
lemon wedges
thinly sliced brown bread and butter

Preparation time: 20–30 minutes
Cooking time: 6–8 minutes

1. Rinse the sardines under a cold tap and pat dry. Cover a grill rack with foil and arrange the sardines on top. Heat the grill.
2. Put a good pinch of salt and a generous grinding of black and white peppers into a bowl. Whisk in the olive oil, then the lemon juice, then add the dried oregano and garlic.
3. Brush each fish with a little of the oil mixture, then cook under a hot grill for 3–4 minutes.
4. Turn the fish over and brush with the remaining mixture, then cook for a further 3–4 minutes until crisp. Serve at once with lemon wedges and thinly sliced brown bread and butter.

ANCHOIADE

This wonderfully piquant anchovy paste has many variations, not only in consistency but in added ingredients also. Black olives, chopped parsley, a pounded tomato and even brandy are sometimes worked into the mixture. The paste is excellent with young beans, or baked potatoes, or with cold meats.

Serves 6–8
2–3 large garlic cloves, peeled
100 g (4 oz) canned anchovies, with their oil
1–2 tablespoons olive oil
1–2 tablespoons lemon juice
freshly ground black pepper
8 thick slices of bread, crusts removed if wished

Preparation time: 5 minutes
Cooking time: 5 minutes
Oven: 220°C, 425°F, Gas Mark 7

1. Crush the garlic cloves until really pulpy in a large mortar and pestle.
2. Chop then pound the anchovy fillets. Mix them with their oil, then gradually beat into the garlic. Add the olive oil, little by little, until the mixture is very thick.
3. Whisk in lemon juice to thin the paste to taste, then sprinkle with freshly ground black pepper.
4. Toast the bread slices on one side only. Spread the untoasted sides with the paste, pressing it in well.
5. Bake in the preheated oven for 3–4 minutes until sizzling hot. Serve the slices whole or cut into fingers, with a chilled wine.

RED MULLET ON FENNEL STALKS
WITH ROUILLE

Serves 6
6 medium red mullet, cleaned, livers reserved
1 bundle dried fennel stalks (about 24)
2 tablespoons olive oil
Maldon or sea salt
freshly ground black pepper
lemon wedges, to serve, optional
For the rouille:
3 garlic cloves, peeled
1–2 red chillies, seeded and coarsely chopped
2 egg yolks
175–250 ml (6–8 fl oz) olive oil
Maldon or sea salt
freshly ground black pepper
lemon juice (optional)

Preparation time: 20 minutes
Cooking time: 15–20 minutes

1. Rinse the mullet and pat dry. Make 2–3 deep slashes into the thickest part of the flesh on either side of each fish. Break one or two of the fennel branches into small pieces and insert in the slashes.
2. Rinse the remaining fennel stalks under cold running water, shaking off the excess – this is to prevent them catching alight while the fish is grilling. Remove the grill rack and make a bed of the fennel in the bottom of the pan.
3. Brush the fish, and the livers, with a little oil, then arrange the fish on the fennel.[A]
4. Heat a small heavy-based frying pan, add the livers and stir-fry for 1–2 minutes until just firm. Transfer to a small bowl and mash.
5. To make the rouille, pound the garlic very thoroughly in a pestle and mortar. Add the chopped chillies and pound to a paste. Now beat in the mashed mullet livers, until smooth and well-blended.
6. Whisk the egg yolks in another large bowl. Whisk in the garlic paste, mixing very well. Add a few drops of olive oil, beating well, then a few more once the first have been absorbed. Keep on adding the oil, a little at a time, as if making mayonnaise, beating constantly and adding more oil only when the previous addition has been amalgamated. The mixture will be very thick, and a beautiful deep pink.
7. Season lightly with salt, generously with pepper and add a few drops of lemon juice if you like, though this is not traditional.[A]
8. About 15–20 minutes before serving, put the fish under a preheated, fairly hot grill and cook for 7–10 minutes each side, until done and nicely crisp. Serve at once with the lemon wedges, if wished, and the rouille handed round separately.

[A] The mullet may be prepared up to 1 hour in advance, covered and kept in a cool place, preferably not in the refrigerator. The rouille can be made up to 24 hours in advance, covered and kept chilled, although if preparing in advance use only 1 chilli because the flavour is absorbed more by the mayonnaise over a longer period and it will be very fiery indeed.

FISH PLAKI

Fish Plaki, or Psari Plaki as it is called in Greece, has a subtle blend of flavours, which strengthens as the dish cools. Rigani is a mixture of dried flowers and leaves of marjoram, which thrives on Greek hillsides – bring some back from your holidays as it is unobtainable elsewhere, oregano is a good substitute.

Serves 4–6
1 kg (2 lb) fish fillets (bass, halibut, cod, haddock or John Dory)
1 large lemon
3 large onions, peeled and finely sliced
2–3 garlic cloves, peeled and finely chopped
¾ teaspoon rigani (see above) or oregano
3 beef steak tomatoes, blanched, skinned and finely sliced
4–5 tablespoons finely chopped fresh parsley
Maldon or sea salt
freshly ground black pepper
6 tablespoons olive oil
300 ml (½ pint) water

Preparation time: 15 minutes
Cooking time: 40–45 minutes
Oven: 180°C, 350°F, Gas Mark 4

1. Cut the fish into fairly thick slices and arrange in an ovenproof dish. Grate the lemon rind evenly over the fish, then peel off all the pith and cut the flesh into slices. Arrange on top of the fish.
2. Lay the onion slices on top, then scatter the garlic and rigani over. Top with the tomatoes and sprinkle over the parsley, salt and lots of black pepper.
3. Mix the oil with the water and pour over the fish. The liquid should just cover all the ingredients so add a little more water if necessary.
4. Bake in the preheated oven for 40–45 minutes or until a fork penetrates down to the bottom very easily. Remove from the oven and cool to room temperature.[A] Serve with a crisp green salad and bread to mop up the juices.

[A] The dish can be prepared up to 24 hours in advance, covered and kept in a cool place, preferably not the refrigerator.

LEFT TO RIGHT: *Red mullet on fennel stalks with rouille; Fish plaki*

CACCIUCCO

This is a marvellously rich and dark fish stew from Italy's north-western coast, made black as night by the squid's ink. It is utterly delicious, easy to make and infinitely variable. Squid, of course, is essential, but crawfish or shrimp could be used instead of prawns.

Serves 6–8
1 kg (2 lb) squid or cuttlefish, uncleaned weight
450 g (1 lb) prawns, cooked but unshelled
450 g (1 lb) red mullet, cleaned but liver, heads and tails
not removed
450 g (1 lb) John Dory, whiting, hake or other white fish
sea or Maldon salt
freshly ground black pepper
175 ml (6 fl oz) olive oil, plus extra for frying bread
2 large onions, peeled and finely chopped
2 celery stalks, sliced
2 carrots, finely sliced lengthways
3 sprigs parsley
2 large garlic cloves, peeled and finely chopped
1 sprig fresh thyme
1 dried red chilli
450 ml (¾ pint) red wine
750 g (1¾ lb) canned tomatoes, coarsely chopped
1.25 litres (2¼ pints) cold water
1 small French loaf, cut into 12 slices

Preparation time: 45 minutes–1¼ hours
Cooking time: 1 hour

1. Clean the squid, reserving the ink sacs (see page 29), or clean the cuttlefish. To clean the cuttlefish, lay on a flat surface, cut off the tentacles and set aside. With a sharp knife, make a slit down one side of the body, then slip out the flat, thin bone. Pull out the head and insides, cut away the ink sac just by the head and reserve in a bowl, then snip off the little bird-like beak and discard, along with the head and entrails. Wash the body thoroughly in running cold water, rubbing off the outer membrane. Rinse the tentacles.
2. Cut the bodies into rings and chop the tentacles. Shell the prawns, reserving the shells and heads. Cut the heads and tails off the mullet, reserving them with the prawn shells, then chop the fish into large chunks. Prepare the remaining fish in the same way, chopping the flesh coarsely and reserving heads (if they have them).
3. Put all the fish into a large bowl and sprinkle with salt, black pepper and 2 tablespoons olive oil. Leave to marinate for 30 minutes.
4. Meanwhile, heat 5 tablespoons oil in a large pan, add the onions, celery, carrots, parsley, garlic, thyme and red chilli and cook very gently for 5 minutes.
5. Add the reserved prawn shells, fish heads and tails and brown over a medium heat. Pour in the wine and boil hard for 3–4 minutes, then simmer for 5–10 minutes

until reduced. Add the ink sacs, crushing them with a wooden spoon to release the ink.
6. Add the tomatoes, with their juice, and the water. Bring to the boil, season lightly with salt and black pepper then cook for 30 minutes. Strain into a bowl pressing the mixture to extract the full flavour.
7. Heat the rest of the oil in another large saucepan, add the squid and cook gently for 15 minutes. Add the prawns and cook for a further 5 minutes, then add the remaining fish, season with salt, black pepper and cook, stirring occasionally, for 10 minutes.
8. Reheat the stock gently in the cleaned pan.
9. Pour 5 cm (2 inches) oil into a pan and heat to 190°C/375°F, or when a cube of stale bread turns golden in 50 seconds. Fry the slices of bread, a few at a time, until golden on both sides. Drain on paper towels and put in the bottom of a large soup tureen or big soup plates.
10. Pile the fish into the tureen or distribute equally between the plates. Boil the stock hard for 10 seconds, then pour over the fish. Serve at once.

CURRIED HADDOCK FRITTERS

A featherlight spicy batter turns haddock (or cod) into an unusual dish. The curry powder not only adds piquancy but helps to draw out the flavour of the fish.

Serves 6
1 kg (2 lb) haddock fillet, skinned
1 × size 1 egg (or 2 × size 4 eggs)
300 ml (½ pint) water
225 g (8 oz) flour
1–2 teaspoons curry powder
Maldon or sea salt
freshly ground black pepper
oil for deep frying
175 ml (6 fl oz) thick mayonnaise
3 tablespoons plain unsweetened yogurt
¼ teaspoon ground turmeric
1 small green chilli, seeded and very finely chopped
lettuce, coriander and lemon slices, to serve

Preparation time: 15 minutes
Cooking time: 15–20 minutes

1. Cut the haddock into bite-sized cubes and dry between paper towels.
2. Whisk the egg until frothy, then beat in the water. Mix well until amalgamated, then gradually sift in the flour, whisking all the time to make a really smooth batter.
3. Add curry powder, salt and pepper and beat again.
4. Fill a deep fat fryer one-third full of oil and heat to a temperature of 190°C/375°F, or until a cube of stale bread turns golden in 50 seconds.
5. Add the fish cubes to the bowl of batter, turning them to coat completely.

6. Add a few cubes to the hot oil and deep fry for 4–5 minutes until golden and puffed. Remove and drain on paper towels and keep warm while frying the rest. (Don't be tempted to fry too many at once or the temperature of the oil will drop.)

7. Mix the mayonnaise, yogurt, turmeric and chopped chilli together in a small bowl, then serve with the fish, accompanied by lemon slices, lettuce and coriander.

FRIED BABY SQUID WITH GARLIC

Squid is one of those creatures of the sea neglected by the English. We fish it in our waters, then export it all to France and Italy, who gratefully receive it, thinking we are mad not to keep it! Don't be put off by the schoolboy ink-stained appearance for squid are tender, tasty and economical indeed.

1.5 kg (3 lb) baby squid, uncleaned weight
6 tablespoons olive oil
3–4 garlic cloves, peeled and very finely chopped
4 tablespoons finely chopped fresh parsley
2–3 tablespoons lemon juice
Maldon or sea salt
freshly ground black pepper

Preparation time: 30 minutes
Cooking time: 20–25 minutes

Curried haddock fritters with mayonnaise; Fried baby squid with garlic

1. To clean the baby squid, first, grasp the tentacles and pull – the head and insides will slip out of the body. Snip the tentacles off just above the head and reserve. If you need the ink for a recipe, carefully detach the ink sac from the head (it is long and narrow, and the ink will show through the thin membrane quite clearly) and drop into a bowl. It's a good idea to do the whole process over a bowl, so that if you do break the sac, it doesn't matter. Frozen squid will often release quite a bit of ink on thawing as the sacs may have been crushed on freezing, in which case pour off into a separate bowl until needed.

2. Discard the head and insides and slip out the fine transparent quill from inside the body – this pulls out easily. Rinse well under cold running water, rubbing off the outer pinky membrane. You now have a smooth pearly body with a fin on each side and the tentacles, all quite edible, and ready for cooking.

3. Slice the bodies into thin rings. Chop the tentacles and keep separate.

4. Heat the oil in a large frying pan, add the rings and cook, stirring fairly frequently, for 10 minutes, then add the tentacles – try and keep them in one half of the pan if you can – and fry for a further 5–10 minutes until cooked and tender. Don't overcook or they'll turn rubbery.

5. Transfer the squid with a slotted spoon into a warmed serving dish, piling the pinky tentacles on top of the body rings. Add the garlic to the pan and stir-fry for 30 seconds. Add the parsley and cook for another few seconds until crisp, then pour over the squid.

6. Sprinkle over the lemon juice, salt and freshly ground black pepper and serve at once, with rice or good crusty bread.

CURRIED PRAWNS AND NOODLES IN COCONUT MILK

In Malaysia coconut milk is used to flavour many dishes. Creamed coconut is available from many supermarkets and good grocers.

Serves 6
1 kg (2 lb) prawns, cooked but unshelled
1 × 5 cm (2 inch) piece lemon rind
1 bay leaf
6 white peppercorns, lightly crushed
3 parsley sprigs
1 litre (1¾ pints) water
2 tablespoons peanut oil
2 large onions, peeled and finely chopped
3 garlic cloves, peeled and finely chopped
¼ teaspoon ground turmeric
1 teaspoon ground coriander
1–2 pinches chilli powder
pinch of ground cardamom
1 × 25 mm (1 inch) piece fresh root ginger, peeled and grated
1 × 7.5 cm (3 inch) block creamed coconut
350 g (12 oz) thin egg noodles
Maldon or sea salt
finely chopped fresh parsley, to garnish

Preparation time: 30 minutes
Cooking time: 50 minutes

1. Peel the prawns, putting the heads and shells into a large pan.
2. Add the lemon rind, bay leaf, peppercorns and parsley sprigs to the pan, together with the water. Bring to the boil, then lower the heat and simmer fairly fast for about 25–30 minutes until the stock is reduced to a scant 600 ml (1 pint).
3. Meanwhile, heat the oil in a large heavy-based pan, add the onions and cook very gently, for about 20 minutes until very soft but not coloured. Stir from time to time to prevent sticking, and keep the pan tightly covered during cooking.
4. Add the garlic, turmeric, coriander, chilli powder, cardamom and grated ginger. Stir well and cook for another 5 minutes.
5. Strain the stock and add to the onions, then stir in the coconut. Bring the liquid to the boil, and bubble for 5–6 minutes until the coconut has completely melted. Simmer fairly fast for another 5 minutes until reduced by about half.
6. Add the noodles and prawns and cook for 4–5 minutes until the noodles are tender but still have some 'bite'. Spoon the mixture into a serving dish or bowl, sprinkle with a little salt and lots of chopped parsley and serve at once.

STEAMED SPICED FISH

Steaming has long been a favourite Chinese method for cooking whole fish. In this dish, Middle meets the Far East, combining the cooking technique of the latter with the traditional spices of the former.

Serves 6
1 × 1.5 kg (3¼–3½ lb) whole bass, bream or grey mullet, cleaned but head and tail left on
1 tablespoon Maldon or sea salt
freshly ground black pepper
1 tablespoon cumin seeds, lightly crushed
5 cm (2 inch) piece fresh root ginger, peeled and finely chopped
2 tablespoons lemon juice
2 tablespoons olive oil
2–3 garlic cloves, peeled and finely chopped
1 tablespoon coriander seeds, crushed
celery leaves, to garnish

Preparation time: 10 minutes, plus standing
Cooking time: 15–25 minutes

1. Rinse the fish in cold water, then rub all over with the salt and lots of black pepper. Leave to stand, at room temperature, for 30 minutes to draw out excess moisture and firm up the flesh.
2. Put the grill rack into a roasting pan, and pour in an inch of boiling water. Set over a low heat so the liquid is gently simmering.
3. Transfer the fish to a heatproof serving plate, discarding any liquid which may have collected around it. Sprinkle on the cumin seeds and ginger, then put the plate on the rack. Cover the whole roasting pan with foil, pressing it around the edges to form as close a seal as possible, then cook for 15–25 minutes until the fish flakes easily. Test it with the point of a sharp knife near the gills so as not to spoil the appearance of the fish.
4. Take off the heat, remove the foil, and sprinkle over the lemon juice.
5. Quickly heat the oil in a small frying pan, add the garlic and coriander seeds and stir-fry over a high heat for about a minute, until the aroma of the spices is quite powerful. Pour the sizzling oil over the fish and serve at once, garnished with celery leaves.

You could cook whole sole, plaice or mackerel in the same way. The flat fish will need a much shorter cooking time – about 6-8 minutes; mackerel will probably take a bit longer, but not more than 15 minutes unless they are very thick. Allow 1 fish for 1-2 people, depending on the size of the fish.

Curried prawns and noodles in coconut milk; Steamed whole spiced fish

TURKISH MACKEREL

One tends to think of mackerel as a particularly English fish, but it is much appreciated in the Mediterranean too, especially in Turkey, where this recipe is popular. The dish is served at room temperature.

Serves 6
2 large mackerel, about 750 g–1 kg (1½–2 lb) in weight each, cleaned but heads and tails left on
6 tablespoons olive oil
3 large onions, peeled and finely sliced
2 green peppers, seeded and finely sliced
4 large garlic cloves, peeled and finely chopped
4 large tomatoes, blanched, skinned and thinly sliced
8 tablespoons finely chopped fresh parsley
2–3 tablespoons tomato purée
pinch of sugar
150 ml (¼ pint) water
Maldon or sea salt
freshly ground black pepper
4–6 tablespoons lemon juice
75 g (3 oz) black olives, stoned

Preparation time: 15 minutes, plus cooling
Cooking time: about 50 minutes

1. Score the mackerel 2–3 times on each side, making diagonal slashes.
2. Heat the oil in a pan large enough to take the fish side by side, then add the mackerel and fry for about 5 minutes, turning once, until browned on both sides. Remove from the pan.
3. Add the onions and cook until soft and lightly coloured, about 10 minutes. Add the green peppers and garlic and fry for another 5 minutes.
4. Put the tomatoes in the pan, scatter over the parsley, then mix the tomato purée and sugar with the water and pour over. Add salt and pepper, then bring the liquid to bubbling point.
5. Turn the heat low and simmer for about 10 minutes, then carefully return the fish to the pan, pushing them slightly into the sauce, so that they are covered. Cook for a further 10 minutes, spooning a little more sauce over them after 5 minutes if necessary.
6. Transfer the mackerel to a serving platter, pour over the sauce, then 4 tablespoons lemon juice. Leave to cool slightly, then taste the sauce and add more lemon juice if needed.
7. Garnish with the black olives and leave to cool completely. Serve the dish at room temperature, cut into thick slices.[A]

[A] May be prepared up to 6 hours in advance, covered and kept chilled, once the fish and sauce are completely cool. Bring to room temperature a good hour before serving.

SQUID IN RED WINE

Serves 4–6
1.5 kg (3 lb) squid, uncleaned weight
4 tablespoons olive oil
2 large onions, peeled and finely chopped
3–4 large garlic cloves, peeled and finely chopped
Maldon or sea salt
freshly ground black pepper
2 sprigs fresh thyme
¼ teaspoon ground cinnamon
pinch of sugar
300 ml (½ pint) red wine
300 ml (½ pint) water
4 tablespoons finely chopped fresh parsley
1 tablespoon chopped celery leaves, to garnish

Preparation time: 30 minutes
Cooking time: 1¼ hours

1. Clean the squid (page 29), discarding the ink sacs or straining the ink and freezing for another dish. Wash the body and tentacles and chop into fine rings.
2. Heat the olive oil in a saucepan, add the onions and sweat for 5 minutes, then add the garlic and chopped squid and cook for another 10 minutes until the onions are quite soft.
3. Add some salt, a fair bit of pepper, the thyme, cinnamon and sugar, then pour in the wine and water. Bring just to the boil, then lower the heat, cover and simmer very gently for about an hour until the squid is absolutely tender and most of the liquid absorbed. If there is still too much liquid, remove the squid with a slotted spoon, then quickly boil until reduced and thickened slightly.
4. Pour the juices over the squid, sprinkle with the parsley and celery and either serve immediately – pasta makes a good accompaniment – or leave to cool to room temperature and serve with a green salad.

SARDINES WITH CUMIN AND GARLIC

Serves 6
12–18 large sardines, thawed if frozen
2–3 tablespoons cumin seeds, lightly crushed
3–5 large garlic cloves, peeled and finely chopped
6 tablespoons finely chopped fresh parsley
Maldon or sea salt
freshly ground black pepper
2 eggs (size 1), beaten
50–75 g (2–3 oz) flour
corn oil, for deep frying
cherry tomatoes and celery leaves, to serve

Preparation time: 30 minutes
Cooking time: 15–25 minutes

CLOCKWISE FROM BOTTOM: *Turkish mackerel; Sardines with cumin and garlic; Squid in red wine*

1. Rinse the sardines, cut off the heads and tails, then split open down the belly. Wash out the insides, then place the fish, skin side up, on a flat surface and press lightly all down the backbone. Turn the fish over and pull the bone out – it should slip away quite easily.

2. Mix the cumin seeds, garlic and parsley together, then add a good pinch of salt and a generous grinding of pepper. Spread the herb and spice mixture thinly on a flat surface, then quickly and lightly dip the sardines, opened flat out and flesh side down, into the herbs. Fold the sardines shut.[A]

3. In a shallow dish, whisk the eggs until frothy, then place the flour on a plate. Holding the sardines shut by their bellies, dip them into the eggs, then roll lightly in the flour.

4. Heat a good 2.5 cm (1 inch) corn oil in a large frying pan, add 3–4 sardines and fry for about 4–5 minutes, turning once, until crisp. Drain on paper towels and keep them warm while cooking the rest. Serve at once with tiny sweet cherry tomatoes and garnish with a few celery leaves.

[A] May be prepared up to 2 hours in advance, covered and kept chilled. Bring to room temperature before continuing with step 3.

BAKED FISH WITH PINE NUT SAUCE

Serves 8–10

1.75 kg (4 lb) sea bream, bass or grey mullet, cleaned
but left whole, or 2 large pieces of fresh cod or haddock
fillet, or 2 × 1 kg (2 lb) dorade
Maldon or sea salt
freshly ground black pepper
6 tablespoons olive oil
For the sauce:
225 g (8 oz) pine nuts
3–4 large garlic cloves, peeled and crushed
freshly ground white pepper
about 6 tablespoons olive oil
about 4 tablespoons lemon juice
1 large curly lettuce, shredded
3 lemons, finely sliced
75 g (3 oz) black olives, stoned
bunch of fresh parsley, finely chopped

Preparation time: 20 minutes, plus chilling and standing
Cooking time: 1–1¼ hours
Oven: 180°C, 350°F, Gas Mark 4

1. Rinse the fish in cold water, then rub it well with salt
and chill for 30 minutes. Bring back to room temperature
for 15 minutes.
2. Sprinkle liberally with black pepper, then brush all
over with oil. Brush a large piece of foil with oil as well,
place the fish on it (if using fillet pieces, place one on top
of the other, skin sides outwards), then fold and seal
tightly (make the seal at the top, so that it can easily be
unwrapped to test if the fish is ready). Place the parcel in
a roasting pan and bake in the preheated oven for 40
minutes to 1 hour, depending on the fish.
3. Test the fish, it should be opaque but firm and flaking
easily. If so, remove from the oven, otherwise give it
another 10–15 minutes.[A]
4. Meanwhile, make the sauce. Grind the pine nuts until
powdery, then pound in a bowl with the garlic. Add salt
and pepper, then stir in 1 tablespoon each of oil and
lemon juice.
5. Gradually add the rest of the oil, beating all the time,
and alternating with a little lemon if the mixture is getting
too thick. It should finally resemble a thick mayonnaise.
Taste, adding more lemon, oil, salt or pepper if needed
and chill until ready to serve.[A]
6. Remove the fish from the foil and place on the lettuce
pouring over any cooking juices.
7. Lay the lemon slices around and over the fish as
wished, then garnish and serve with the sauce.

[A] The fish may be baked up to 8 hours in advance and
left to cool, in the foil. Chill once cool and bring back to
room temperature for at least 1 hour before serving.
[A] The sauce may be made the day before and kept in a
screw-top jar, chilled, until ready to be served.

SPICY FISH BALLS

*Fish fingers are not a new idea – the Middle East has had
them for centuries. But their finely minced and highly
spiced rissoles, round patties or little balls are a far cry
from our Western version!*

Serves 4–6

1 kg (2 lb) sea bream, bass, haddock, cod or halibut,
skinned and filleted
50 g (2 oz) fresh breadcrumbs
1 large onion, peeled and minced or grated
2 garlic cloves, peeled and finely chopped
Maldon or sea salt
freshly ground white pepper
6 tablespoons finely chopped fresh parsley
1 teaspoon coriander seeds, ground or ½ teaspoon
ground coriander
1 teaspoon dill seeds, crushed
1 egg (size 1)
flour, for dusting
corn oil, for frying
3 tablespoons lemon juice
½ teaspoon ground cinnamon
lemon wedges, to serve

Preparation time: 30 minutes
Cooking time: 10–20 minutes

1. Cut the fish into large chunks and either put through
the fine blade of a mincer or chop finely in a food
processor.
2. Soak the breadcrumbs in cold water for 5 minutes,
then squeeze dry and place in a bowl. Add the fish, with
the onion, garlic, a good seasoning of salt and pepper and
4 tablespoons of the parsley. Mix well.
3. Mix the coriander and dill seeds with the egg and beat
into the fish mixture, working it to a really smooth paste.
Take walnut-sized lumps of the fish and, keeping your
hands moistened with cold water, roll into small balls.
4. Sprinkle a few tablespoons of flour on a dry, flat
surface and quickly roll the fish balls in it – do not make
them too floury.[A]
5. Heat a good 1 cm (½ inch) oil in a large frying pan,
and add as many fish balls as will comfortably fit, leaving
room to turn them. Cook gently for 6–10 minutes,
turning 2–3 times until they are nicely golden and crisp
on the outside. Keep warm while cooking the remainder.
6. Pile into a serving dish, sprinkle with lemon juice, the
rest of the parsley and the cinnamon and serve at once
with lemon wedges.

[A] May be prepared up to 6 hours ahead, covered and
chilled. Bring to room temperature before cooking.

Baked fish with pine nut sauce; Spicy fish balls

MONKFISH IN CHILLI-BASIL SAUCE

It is essential that the basil be fresh for this wonderful sweet-hot sauce, but fresh tarragon, coriander or frozen mint can be used instead should fresh basil be unobtainable.

Serves 6
1.5 kg (3–3¼ lb) tailpiece monkfish
4 tablespoons olive oil
Maldon or sea salt
freshly ground black pepper
For the sauce:
2 tablespoons olive oil
1 Spanish onion, peeled and very finely chopped
2 garlic cloves, peeled and very finely chopped
1–2 small green chillies, seeded and very finely chopped
400 g (14 oz) canned tomatoes
8–10 fresh basil leaves, very finely chopped
freshly ground white pepper
¼ teaspoon ground cinnamon
fresh red and green chillies, to garnish

Preparation time: 15 minutes
Cooking time: 40 minutes

1. Fillet the monkfish into 2 large triangular pieces (page 73). Sprinkle with the oil, a little salt and lots of pepper, then leave to stand at room temperature while making the sauce.
2. Heat the oil in a large pan, add the onion and garlic and sweat gently for 5 minutes, then cover with a butter paper (page 7), put on the lid and cook gently for 25 minutes until the onions are very soft and mushy, adding the chillies for the last 5 minutes (earlier for real spice lovers!).
3. Purée the tomatoes, with their juice, in a blender or food processor, until very smooth, then add to the pan. Stir well then simmer, uncovered, for 10 minutes to reduce and thicken slightly.
4. About 5 minutes before the sauce is ready, cook the fish under a preheated, very hot grill, for 2½–3½ minutes each side until just done – it should be very slightly undercooked in the middle. Transfer to a warmed serving dish.
5. Stir the basil, salt, white pepper and cinnamon into the sauce, boil fast for 30 seconds, then pour over the fish and serve at once, garnished with chillies.

Monkfish in chilli-basil sauce; Devilled kipper tart

DEVILLED KIPPER TART

An unusual and excellent tart, the sweet-spicy pastry combines well with the smokiness of the kippers.

Serves 4–6
175 g (6 oz) wholemeal flour
1 teaspoon baking powder
25 g (1 oz) ground almonds
2 teaspoons curry powder
90 g (3½ oz) unsalted butter, diced
about 1 tablespoon chilled water
For the filling:
40 g (1½ oz) unsalted butter
pinch of ground cumin
1 teaspoon turmeric
¼ teaspoon cayenne pepper
pinch of ground cinnamon
3–4 tablespoons lemon juice
400 g (14 oz) kipper fillets, skinned, boned and flaked
120 ml (4 fl oz) fromage blanc
3 tablespoons finely chopped fresh parsley
lemon slices, to garnish

Preparation time: 35 minutes, plus cooling
Cooking time: 25–30 minutes
Oven: 220°C, 425°F, Gas Mark 7

1. Make the pastry. Sift the flour with the baking powder, ground almonds and curry powder, then crumble in the butter and rub through your fingers until the mixture has the consistency of fine breadcrumbs.
2. Add the water and mix to a stiff dough, then roll into a ball on a lightly floured surface. Flatten slightly, then roll out into a circle to fit a 20 cm (8 inch) sandwich tin.
3. Line the tin with non-stick silicone paper, then line with the pastry. Line the base of the pastry with foil and beans and bake in the preheated oven for 15 minutes. Remove the beans and foil, and cook for a further 8–10 minutes or until the pastry is crisp and lightly golden. Remove from the oven and cool in the tin, then carefully transfer the case to a serving plate. (For a picnic, leave in the tin for ease of transporting.) [A]
4. Meanwhile make the filling. Melt the butter in a frying pan, add the cumin, turmeric, cayenne pepper and cinnamon and stir-fry for 1 minute, then add the lemon juice and kipper fillets and cook for about 5 minutes, stirring constantly. Take off the heat and cool slightly.
5. Mix the kippers with the fromage blanc, then spoon into the pastry case. Sprinkle with parsley, garnish with lemon slices and serve at room temperature.[A]

[A] The case may be cooked up to 4 days in advance and kept in an airtight tin. The filling may be prepared one day in advance but do not fill the case until just before serving. Keep the filling chilled and bring to room temperature about 1 hour before you want to use it.

BRAISED COD IN BLACK BEAN SAUCE

The black bean sauce gives a deliciously nutty, salty flavour to this cod dish. Black beans are easily obtainable in oriental food stores where they are usually sold as 'black beans in salted sauce'.

Serves 6
6 cod steaks, each about 175–225 g (6–8 oz) in weight
2 tablespoons soy sauce
3 tablespoons dry sherry
2 tablespoons peanut or grapeseed oil
2 garlic cloves, peeled and crushed
1 × 5 cm (2 inch) piece fresh root ginger, peeled and finely chopped
3 tablespoons black bean sauce
3 spring onions, green tops only, finely shredded
¼ teaspoon ground cinnamon
175 ml (6 fl oz) fish stock

*Preparation time: 5 minutes, plus marinating
Cooking time: 30–35 minutes*

1. Rinse the cod steaks and pat dry. Put in a shallow dish and spoon over the soy sauce and sherry. Leave for 30 minutes at room temperature, turning them once.
2. Heat the oil in 1 or 2 frying pans. (The fish should lie in a single layer.) Add the garlic and ginger and stir-fry for about 30 seconds, then add the black bean sauce, spring onion tops and cinnamon and mix together well.
3. Add the cod, with their marinade, to the pan and brown on both sides over a high heat, about 2 minutes.
4. Add the stock, turn the heat down slightly, bring the liquid to the boil, then simmer over the lowest possible heat for 15–20 minutes until the fish is just done. Add a little extra stock or water if it seems to be getting too dry – the fish should be coated in a little thick sauce, rather than swimming in liquid. Serve at once, or leave to cool to room temperature and serve cold.

FISH SUPPERS

GREY MULLET WITH HERBS

Serves 6
3 grey mullet, each about 450 g (1 lb) in weight, scaled
and cleaned but left whole, and roes left in
Maldon or sea salt
1 tablespoon vinegar (optional)
6–8 tablespoons olive oil
2–3 garlic cloves, peeled and finely chopped
4 tablespoons finely chopped fresh parsley
3 tablespoons finely chopped fresh coriander leaves
1 tablespoon finely chopped fresh marjoram
600 ml (1 pint) fish stock (page 7)
3–4 tablespoons lemon juice
¼ teaspoon ground cinnamon
freshly ground black pepper
lemon slices and coriander, to garnish

Preparation time: 15 minutes, plus standing and cooling
Cooking time: 30–35 minutes (excluding the fish stock)
Oven: 180°C, 350°F, Gas Mark 4

1. If you have caught the fish yourself, or know they have
been locally caught near a port, then soak for 5 minutes
in lightly salted and vinegared water (1 teaspoon each to
600 ml (1 pint) cold water). Rinse the fish and repeat
twice with fresh salt, vinegar and water. This will remove
the slightly muddy taste. Mullet from the fishmonger
(usually from deep-sea waters) merely need to be
rubbed with a good bit of salt, then left for 30 minutes.
Rinse off excess salt and pat dry with paper towels.
2. Heat 6 tablespoons of the oil in a roasting pan over a
medium heat, add the fish and fry for 3–4 minutes on
each side until browned. Remove then add the garlic and
parsley and fry for 1–2 minutes until lightly crisp.
3. Drain off the oil, return the fish to the pan then
sprinkle over the remaining oil, the rest of the herbs and
the fish stock. Add a little salt and bake, uncovered, in the
preheated oven for 15–25 minutes until firm and just
done. Test near the gills for easy flaking.
4. Remove from the oven, sprinkle over 3 tablespoons
lemon juice and the cinnamon, stirring it lightly into the
liquid. Taste and add extra lemon juice if necessary, then a
liberal grinding of pepper. Garnish and serve hot or leave to
cool to room temperature.

Grey mullet with herbs; Salmon and almond quiche

SALMON AND ALMOND QUICHE

Serves 4–6
225 g (8 oz) made weight shortcrust pastry, thawed if
frozen
flour, for dusting
50 g (2 oz) ground almonds
1 × 225 g (8 oz) can red salmon, drained and flaked
freshly grated nutmeg
2–3 drops Tabasco
3 egg yolks (size 1)
1 egg (size 1)
300 ml (½ pint) double cream
Maldon or sea salt
freshly ground white pepper
2 tablespoons olive oil
25 g (1 oz) blanched flaked almonds
3–4 tablespoons finely chopped fresh parsley, plus a
sprig, to garnish

Preparation time: 15 minutes
Cooking time: 30 minutes
Oven: 200°C, 400°F, Gas Mark 6;
then 180°C, 350°F, Gas Mark 4

1. Place a baking sheet in the preheated oven.
2. Roll out the pastry on a lightly floured board to a
circle 28 cm (11 inches) in diameter. Line a quiche or flan
tin 23 cm (9 inches) in diameter with non-stick silicone
paper and cover with the pastry, gently easing it into the
tin. Trim and lightly prick the bottom all over with a fork.
3. Mix the ground almonds into the salmon, add a good
grating of nutmeg and a few drops of Tabasco, then beat
in the egg yolks and whole egg, mixing well.
4. Stir the cream into the egg mixture, season with salt
and pepper, then pour into the pastry case.
5. Bake in the preheated oven on the hot baking sheet
for 20 minutes, then lower the heat and cook for another
10 minutes until puffed up and lightly golden on top.
6. Five minutes before the quiche is ready, heat the oil in
a small frying pan, add the almonds and stir-fry for 1–2
minutes until deep gold but take care not to burn them.
Remove and drain on paper towels, then sprinkle with
salt. Mix with the parsley while the nuts are still warm.
7. Remove the quiche from the oven, remove the paper
and place the quiche on a dish. Sprinkle with almonds
and parsley, garnish and serve hot, warm or cold.

FISH AND COURGETTE MOUSSAKA

Serves 6

1.25–1.5 kg (2½–3 lb) fish, preferably a mixture of cod,
haddock, bream or bass plus 1 mackerel or red mullet,
all trimmings, bones and skins reserved
Maldon or sea salt
freshly ground black pepper
1 celery stalk, sliced
1 carrot, sliced lengthways
1 leek, sliced into rings
6 white peppercorns, lightly crushed
3 parsley sprigs
2 thyme sprigs
1 tablespoon wine vinegar
1 litre (1¾ pints) water
60 g (2½ oz) unsalted butter
3 tablespoons flour
freshly grated nutmeg
2 tablespoons olive oil
1 large onion, peeled and finely sliced
3 large garlic cloves, peeled and finely chopped
2 tablespoons finely chopped fresh mint
2 tablespoons finely chopped fresh parsley
¼ teaspoon sugar
freshly ground allspice
1 × 400 g (14 oz) can plum tomatoes, drained and
coarsely chopped
6 medium courgettes, trimmed and thickly sliced
6 tablespoons dried breadcrumbs
6 tablespoons grated Parmesan cheese
mint sprigs, to garnish

Preparation time: 30–40 minutes
Cooking time: about 1½ hours
Oven: 180°C, 350°F, Gas Mark 4

1. Cut the fish into large cubes, put on a shallow dish,
sprinkle with salt and pepper and reserve.
2. To make the stock, put the trimmings, bones and skin
into a large saucepan with the celery, carrot, leek,
peppercorns, herbs and vinegar, then add the cold water.
Bring to the boil, simmer gently for 20 minutes, then
strain into a jug. Return to the rinsed-out pan and reduce
by hard boiling to about 600 ml (1 pint).[F]
3. Melt 40 g (1½ oz) of the butter in a small pan, then stir
in the flour. Cook for 1–2 minutes, remove from the heat,
then gradually add a little fish stock, stirring to make a
thick paste. Continue to add the stock, little by little, and
always stirring until all is incorporated. Return to the heat
and stir until it begins to thicken, 5–7 minutes.
4. Bring the sauce to bubbling point, season with salt,
pepper and lots of nutmeg, then let it simmer gently for
about 20 minutes, until nicely thickened and highly
flavoured. Stir it from time to time to stop a skin forming.
5. Heat the oil in another large pan, add the onion and
garlic and sweat for about 15 minutes until softened. Put

in an ovenproof dish and then arrange the fish on top.
6. Add the mint and parsley to the pan and stir-fry for 1
minute, then sprinkle with the sugar and allspice and add
the tomatoes, crushing them slightly with the back of a
wooden spoon. Add 2 tablespoons of the sauce, stirring
well, then simmer for 10–15 minutes until the tomatoes
are thick. Pour all over the fish.
7. Heat the remaining butter in a frying pan, add the
courgettes and quickly fry for 1 minute, turning constantly, until lightly browned. Spread over the tomatoes, then
pour in the sauce to just cover the courgettes. (Any
leftover sauce can be frozen and used for other dishes.)
8. Sprinkle over the breadcrumbs and cheese and bake
in the preheated oven for 25–30 minutes until the top is
bubbling and deep golden. Serve at once.

[F] Freeze the stock for 3–4 weeks. Thaw gently in a
saucepan over moderate heat.
[M] To defrost the stock in the microwave, turn into a
large bowl and heat on Maximum (Full) for 10–15
minutes, breaking up and stirring as required.

KIPPER PILAU

2 large kippers, on the bone
3 tablespoons olive oil
1 large onion, peeled and finely chopped
¼ teaspoon turmeric
¼ teaspoon ground cinnamon
300 g (11 oz) long-grain rice
finely ground sea salt
freshly ground black pepper
50 g (2 oz) sultanas
25 g (1 oz) flaked almonds
4 tablespoons finely chopped fresh parsley, to garnish

Preparation time: 15 minutes
Cooking time: 35–40 minutes

1. Put the kippers, head down, into a large jug and pour
in boiling water, so that the kippers are completely
submerged. Cover and leave for 10 minutes.
2. Meanwhile, heat 2 tablespoons of the oil in a large
pan, add the onion, cover and fry gently for 10 minutes
until softened. Add the turmeric and cinnamon and cook
for another 1 minute.
3. Pour the rice into a measuring jug and note the
volume. Transfer it to a sieve and pour boiling water
over, stir once or twice, then rinse under cold running
water until the water runs clear. Add to the pan and stir
until all the grains are coated with oil.
4. Drain the kippers, pouring the water into a jug. Pour
the same volume of water as rice into the pan and bring
to the boil. While the rice is coming to the boil, quickly
cut off the heads and tails of the kippers, lift out the large
bones and flake the flesh into bite-sized pieces. Add to

the rice, stirring once, season lightly with salt and generously with pepper, then stir in the sultanas. Once boiling, reduce the heat, cover and simmer, for about 20 minutes until the rice has absorbed all the liquid and is tender but not mushy. Turn off the heat and leave, still covered, while frying the almonds.

5. Heat the remaining oil in a small frying pan, add the almonds and stir-fry for 2 minutes until golden. Drain, and sprinkle with salt.

6. Pile the pilau on to a warmed serving dish, sprinkle with parsley and almonds and serve at once.

SMOKED HADDOCK WITH RED PEPPER SAUCE

Serves 4–6
450 g (1 lb) smoked haddock fillets
600 ml (1 pint) milk
2 tablespoons olive oil
3 shallots, peeled and finely chopped
2–3 garlic cloves, peeled and finely chopped
2 large red peppers, cored, seeded and finely sliced
4 tablespoons soured cream
150 ml (5 fl oz) low-fat soft cheese
1 tablespoon finely chopped fresh tarragon
freshly ground black pepper
¼–½ teaspoon caster sugar (optional)
250 g (9 oz) pasta bows or shells
25 g (1 oz) butter

Preparation time: 15 minutes
Cooking time: 25–30 minutes

1. Rinse the haddock in cold water, then pour boiling water over it and leave for 2 minutes. Rinse again, then put into a pan, cover with the milk and bring to the boil. Reduce the heat and simmer gently for 10–15 minutes until the fish flakes easily. Strain, reserving the milk, and leave the fish until cool enough to handle easily.

2. Heat the oil in another pan, add the shallots and garlic and fry gently for 5 minutes until softened. Add the peppers and cook gently for 5–6 minutes, stirring occasionally to prevent them sticking.

3. Stir 120 ml (4 fl oz) of the strained milk into the soured cream, then mix in the cheese. Add another tablespoon or so of milk if the mixture seems very thick, it should be the consistency of double cream.

4. Purée the peppers with the cheese mixture in a liquidizer or food processor or simply stir the cream into the peppers, but do make sure that the peppers have been very finely sliced. Return to the pan and add the tarragon and peppers. (Salt will probably be unnecessary since the haddock is very salty.)

5. Taste the sauce, and add a little sugar if necessary. Simmer gently.

6. Bring the remaining milk to the boil in a large pan. Add the pasta and boil for 6–8 minutes until al dente.

7. While the pasta is cooking, skin, bone and flake the fish. Add to the sauce, stirring well to mix.

8. Strain the pasta, return to the pan with half the butter and toss to coat.

9. Over a medium-high heat, whisk the rest of the butter into the sauce. Pile the pasta into a hot serving dish, pour the sauce over and serve at once.

LEFT TO RIGHT: *Fish and courgette moussaka; Kipper pilau; Smoked haddock with red pepper sauce*

FISH RISOTTO

There are many versions of risotto – the one constant is saffron, to add a delicate flavour and lightly tint it gold. Otherwise it is a marvellously flexible dish and may be made with meat, poultry or fish. Shellfish and/or mussels are commonly found in Italy, but for a simpler recipe you can use a mixture of white fish, plus a few prawns and a highly flavoured fish such as red mullet. If you wish to add mussels, scrub them well and debeard them (discarding any that don't close of course), then steam them open during the last 5–6 minutes of cooking, placing them on top of the rice. Just before serving, remove any that have not opened.

Serves 6–8
275 g (10 oz) cooked unshelled prawns
50–75 g (2–3 oz) unsalted butter
1 large onion, peeled and finely chopped
1.2–1.5 litres (2–2½ pints) fish stock (page 7)
1 celery stalk, sliced
1 thyme sprig
2 parsley sprigs
1 mace blade
1 small onion, peeled but left whole
2 cloves
350–450 g (12 oz–1 lb) round-grain rice (e.g. Arborio)
150 ml (¼ pint) dry white wine
450 g (1 lb) monkfish, haddock, halibut or other firm white fillets, skinned and cubed
2 small red mullet, heads and tails removed, cut into 25 mm (1 inch) slices (optional)
3–4 strands saffron
1 garlic clove, peeled and finely chopped
Maldon or sea salt
freshly ground white pepper
40 g (1½ oz) grated Parmesan cheese, plus extra to serve
finely chopped fresh parsley, to garnish

Preparation time: 20 minutes
Cooking time: 45–55 minutes (excluding the fish stock)

1. If you wish, you can shell the prawns, adding the heads and shells to the fish stock to give a richer flavour. But many people prefer to keep the prawns whole and shell them at the table.
2. Heat 25 g (1 oz) of the butter in a large, heavy-based pan, add the onion and sweat gently for 5–10 minutes until soft but not coloured.
3. Meanwhile, put the fish stock, with the prawn shells if adding, into another pan, then tie the celery, thyme, parsley, mace blade and onion studded with the cloves, in a muslin and add to the pan (you don't have to enclose the herbs and spices but it makes it easier when adding the stock to the risotto). Bring just to boiling point, then keep at a gentle simmer, and have a ladle or small

heatproof jug at hand for adding it to the rice.
4. Add the rice (use a larger amount if omitting the mullet) to the onions, and stir until well coated with the butter. Pour in the wine, raise the heat a little and cook for 3–4 minutes until the wine has almost evaporated.
5. Add a ladleful, or about 125 ml (4 fl oz), of the hot stock to the pan and cook on a low heat for 2–4 minutes, until the stock is almost all absorbed, then add another ladleful, stirring into the rice. Keep your eye on the rice and continue adding the stock, a little at a time, and stirring frequently to prevent sticking, until you have added about 1 litre (1¾ pints). By this time, you should be stirring almost constantly.
6. Add the monkfish and red mullet slices, if using, then a little more stock and cook for 4–5 minutes.
7. Put the saffron in a small bowl, pour over 3–4 tablespoons of the stock, stir quickly to start the colour running, then leave.
8. Melt 15 g (½ oz) of the butter in another small pan, add the garlic and prawns and cook for 3–4 minutes, then stir into the risotto. Add the saffron liquid, and another ladleful of stock if you have used the whole quantity of rice. The rice should be tender and the risotto creamily moist without being 'gluey', so be careful at this stage – it is easy to make it too liquid. Season, fairly generously, with salt and pepper.
9. Add the remaining butter and the Parmesan, stirring until melted, then pile into warmed serving dish, sprinkle with parsley and serve at once with extra Parmesan.

MULLET AND BACON KEBABS

Traditionally grey mullet are cooked with bacon and sage, a little cream often being added in their native West Country. For a quick summer supper, these kebabs are delicious and simple to make. If you like the idea of the Cornish accompaniment, bring 4 tablespoons double cream to the boil just before the mullet are ready and dribble over the skewers before serving.

Serves 6
3 grey mullet, about 500 g (1¼ lb) each in weight, cleaned
4 tablespoons olive oil
225 g (8 oz) streaky bacon rashers, rinded
2 tablespoons finely chopped fresh sage leaves
1–2 garlic cloves, peeled and finely chopped
Maldon or sea salt
freshly ground black pepper
lemon wedges, to serve

Preparation time: 20 minutes
Cooking time: 7–12 minutes

1. To fillet grey mullet or any other round-bodied fish, cut off the head and place the fish on a damp cloth to

Fish risotto

prevent it slipping. With a slim-bladed sharp knife, slit along the backbone, from head to tail, then slip the knife underneath the flesh, keeping as near to the bone as possible, sweeping down to the belly, and slitting through it. Cut off at the tail end and pull off the fillet. Repeat with the other side, then skin the fillets and cut the flesh into large chunks. Put in a dish and pour over the olive oil.

2. Cut the bacon rashers into squares. Pound the sage with the garlic and a good pinch of salt in a mixing bowl.

3. Thread the fish, reserving the oil, and bacon on to 6 skewers, starting with bacon, using 2 squares every now and again if necessary between 2 cubes of mullet.

4. Rub a little of the sage and garlic mixture over the fish, then sprinkle with pepper. Drizzle over the olive oil.

5. Cook under a preheated very hot grill for 7–12 minutes, turning every 2 minutes until the fish is done and the bacon crisp. Serve immediately with lemon.

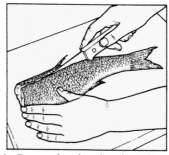

1. Remove head and make a slit along the backbone from head to tail.

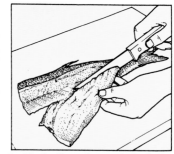

2. Slip knife underneath the flesh keeping near the bone. Cut through skin along belly to free the fillet.

WALNUT-STUFFED HADDOCK

Serves 6
225 g (8 oz) dried green flageolet beans soaked
overnight, or 1 × 450 g (1 lb) can flageolet beans
few celery leaves, or 1 small celery stalk, chopped
Maldon or sea salt
freshly ground black pepper
2 large fillets haddock, each about 350 g (12 oz) in
weight, skinned
50 g (2 oz) unsalted butter
1 medium onion, peeled and finely chopped
4 tablespoons finely chopped fresh parsley
¼ teaspoon fennel seeds, lightly crushed
50 g (2 oz) walnuts, finely chopped
75 g (3 oz) fresh breadcrumbs
1 tablespoon lemon juice
1 egg yolk (size 1)
freshly ground white pepper
pinch of cayenne pepper
2–3 tablespoons olive oil
2 tablespoons lemon juice
To finish and garnish:
2 beef tomatoes, finely sliced
1 onion, peeled and finely sliced
lemon slices
celery leaves

*Preparation time: 15 minutes, plus soaking overnight
(for dried beans)
Cooking time: 35 minutes, plus 1½ hours for dried beans
Oven: 170°C, 325°F, Gas Mark 3*

1. If using dried beans, drain and rinse well, then put in
a large pan, well covered with fresh cold water. Add the
celery and bring slowly to the boil. Simmer gently for 1–
1½ hours until tender but not mushy, sprinkling with a
little salt once the beans are soft.[A]
2. When the beans are softening but not quite done, rub
salt and a good bit of pepper into the fish fillets and leave
aside while making the stuffing.
3. To make the stuffing, melt 25 g (1 oz) of the butter in a
large frying pan, add the onion and sweat for about 5
minutes, then add the parsley, fennel seeds and the
chopped walnuts and stir for another 2 minutes. Tip into
a large bowl.
4. Add the breadcrumbs and lemon juice to the bowl,
then beat in the egg yolk, and season with plenty of salt
and white pepper and just a touch of cayenne.
5. Grease a shallow ovenproof dish which will hold the
fish with enough room to take the beans at the sides.
Alternatively, if you wish to transfer the fish once cooked
to a serving dish, then grease a dish which holds the fish
snugly. Put one fillet on the bottom, spread the stuffing all
over and cover with the second fillet. Cover with a butter
paper and bake, in the preheated oven, for 20–25
minutes until the fish is done.

6. Drain the beans as soon as they are done, or put the
canned beans into a saucepan with their liquid and bring
rapidly to the boil, then simmer for 3–4 minutes until
hot, then drain. Tip the beans into a bowl, sprinkle with
the oil and lemon juice and season lightly with black
pepper.
7. Remove the fish from the oven, either transfer to a
serving dish or leave in the casserole, then arrange the
beans around the fish. Very quickly melt the remaining
butter and when frothy, pour over the fish.
8. Put the sliced tomatoes on the beans, add the onion
slices, then overlap the lemon slices down the centre of
the fish and serve immediately.

[A] The beans may be cooked up to 6 hours before,
drained, covered again in salted cold water and kept
chilled. Bring a large pan of water to the boil just before
serving, add the drained beans and simmer for 2 minutes
to warm through, then garnish as in the recipe.

POACHED SMOKED HADDOCK WITH CORIANDER SEEDS

Serves 4–6
750 g–1 kg (1½–2 lb) smoked haddock, skinned
2 tablespoons olive oil
2 large onions, peeled and finely sliced
1–2 garlic cloves, peeled and crushed
1 tablespoon coriander seeds, lightly crushed
600–900 ml (1–1½ pints) milk
freshly ground allspice
freshly ground black pepper
1 × 350 g (12 oz) can petit pois, drained
4 tablespoons double cream
Continental parsley, to garnish

*Preparation time: 5–10 minutes
Cooking time: 1 hour*

1. Put the fish into a large shallow dish, pour over boiling
water and leave for 2 minutes, then drain and refresh in
fresh cold water.
2. Heat the oil in a large heavy-based saucepan, add the
onions and sweat gently for about 15 minutes until nicely
softened and lightly golden.
3. Add the garlic and coriander seeds and cook for a
further 5 minutes.
4. Pour in the milk and bring slowly to the boil, then add
the fish, pushing it well down in the pan and spooning
some of the milk over if necessary. Cover the pan and
cook for 25–30 minutes, spooning the liquid over the fish
and turning it after 10–15 minutes. Remove the haddock
– using an expanding fish slice if possible to keep it in
one piece – on to a warmed serving platter. Keep warm
by first covering the dish with foil and then carefully

placing it over a saucepan of gently simmering water.
5. Season the milk with allspice and a generous amount of pepper, then add the peas and cook rapidly for 5 minutes, to heat the peas and slightly reduce the milk. If there is still a lot of liquid left, you can drain some off if you wish (keep it for enriching another dish), then stir in the cream and boil for 1 minute. Pour the sauce over the fish, garnish and serve immediately.

MARINATED MONKFISH GRILLED WITH HERBS

Serves 6
1.5 kg (3–3½ lb) tailpiece monkfish
100 ml (3½ fl oz) olive oil
2 tablespoons lemon juice
2–3 garlic cloves, peeled and finely chopped
3 sprigs fresh thyme, leaves stripped from the stems
4 tablespoons finely chopped fresh chives
4 tablespoons finely chopped fresh mint
Maldon or sea salt
freshly ground black pepper
2 tablespoons cognac
mint leaves, to garnish

Preparation time: 10 minutes, plus marinating
Cooking time: 5–9 minutes

1. Fillet the monkfish into 2 long triangular pieces (see page 73) and place in a large shallow dish. Pour over the oil, lemon juice and garlic and leave, covered but not chilled, for 1 hour.[A]
2. Mix the herbs with a good pinch of salt and lots of pepper, then remove the fish from its marinade and sprinkle half the herb mixture over one side of each fillet.
3. Brush the grid of the grill with oil. Put the fillets on the grid, sprinkle with half the cognac and cook under a very hot grill for 2½–4 minutes, depending on the thickness of the fish and how well done you like it.
4. Turn the fillets over, brush with a little of the oil, then spread the remaining herbs over the fish and sprinkle on the rest of the brandy. Cook for another 2½–4 minutes, then garnish and serve. A good salad and tiny new potatoes are the only accompaniments needed.

[A] May be prepared up to 8 hours ahead, covered and chilled. Bring to room temperature before cooking.

CLOCKWISE FROM TOP: *Walnut-stuffed haddock; Marinated monkfish grilled with herbs; Poached smoked haddock with coriander seeds*

LAYERED FISH PIE

In this pie the fish is set in a light creamy custard.

Serves 6
450 g (1 lb) firm white fish fillets, e.g. cod or haddock
1 bay leaf
6 white peppercorns
1.2 litres (2 pints) milk
2 tablespoons olive oil
2 large onions, peeled and finely sliced
450 g (1 lb) potatoes, finely sliced
2 garlic cloves, peeled
ground nutmeg
finely ground sea salt
freshly ground black pepper
6 large eggs
450 g (1 lb) tomatoes, finely sliced
½ teaspoon dried dill
50 g (2 oz) Cheddar or Lancashire cheese, grated
fresh dill, to garnish

Layered fish pie; Omelette Arnold Bennett; Anchovy and pine nut fettucine

*Preparation time: 20–25 minutes
Cooking time: about 40 minutes
Oven: 180°C, 350°F, Gas Mark 4*

1. Rinse the fish in cold water and put into a shallow pan with the bay leaf, peppercorns and half the milk. Bring to the boil and simmer gently, covered, for 15 minutes or until the fish flakes easily.
2. In another pan, heat the oil, add the onions and fry gently for 15 minutes until softened and lightly golden. Remove from the pan with a slotted spoon and reserve.
3. Put the potatoes in layers in a saucepan, sprinkling each layer with a few slivers from one of the garlic cloves, nutmeg, salt and pepper. Cover with the remaining milk, bring to the boil, then simmer gently for about 8–10 minutes until they are just done.
4. Put 4 eggs into a small pan, cover with water and boil until hard; about 10 minutes.

5. Rub an ovenproof casserole with the remaining garlic clove and spoon the onions into the bottom to make a layer. Remove the fish with a slotted spoon and arrange on top of the onions. Strain the milk from the fish and reserve.

6. Add the tomatoes to the oil left in the onion pan and stir-fry over a high heat for 2–3 minutes until beginning to soften and exude a little liquid.

7. Arrange the tomatoes on top of the fish and sprinkle with the dill. Bury the garlic clove used to rub around the casserole into the mixture.

8. Drain the potatoes, reserving the milk. Cool the eggs under cold running water, then shell and slice. Arrange a layer of egg slices over the tomatoes, then cover with the potatoes, in a layer.[A]

9. Beat the remaining 2 eggs well, then whisk into the milk. Pour over the dish, adding a little extra milk if necessary, so that the liquid is level with the potatoes. Sprinkle the cheese on top.

10. Cook in the preheated oven for 12–20 minutes until the 'custard' is very lightly set – you don't want it too solid or the pie will be dry. Garnish with a sprig of dill and serve immediately.

[A] The pie can be prepared up to this stage, covered and kept in a cool place, for up to 8 hours. Reheat the milk to simmering point before beating in the eggs and add 3–4 tablespoons single cream, so that the custard does not set before the ingredients have become really hot.

OMELETTE ARNOLD BENNETT

The famous Edwardian novelist and theatre critic, Arnold Bennett used to dine at the Savoy Hotel several times a week, after seeing a play – and before writing his criticism. This omelette was specially created for him and remains a classic. A crisp green salad and a chilled wine make this the perfect supper.

1 Finnan haddock
600 ml (1 pint) milk
4 tablespoons Parmesan cheese
6 eggs (size 1)
Maldon or sea salt
freshly ground black pepper
25 g (1 oz) butter
4 tablespoons double cream
fresh dill, to garnish

*Preparation time: 5–10 minutes
Cooking time: 25 minutes*

1. Rinse the haddock in cold water, then put into a large pan, cover with the milk and bring to the boil over a fairly low heat. Simmer for 10–15 minutes until the fish just flakes easily. Remove from the pan, (keep the milk for making soup, if you wish), then skin and flake the fish.

2. Mix the fish with the cheese and keep aside.

3. Whisk the eggs until frothy, season lightly with salt and generously with pepper. Melt the butter in a large frying pan and when it is just bubbling pour in the eggs. Cook over a high heat, tilting the pan sideways and lifting the eggs at the edges slightly to let raw egg run underneath.

4. When almost cooked but still liquid on top, spread over the fish mixture. Pour on the double cream, then put under a preheated hot grill for 1–2 minutes until bubbling and slightly golden. Garnish and serve at once.

ANCHOVY AND PINE NUT FETTUCINE

Canned anchovies are a very useful storecupboard standby. Not only can they lift meat casseroles and gravies (they were frequently used with meat in British cookery hundreds of years ago), but combined with cream, soft cheeses or yogurt and nuts they make a quick, economical and delicious sauce for pasta. Hazelnuts can be substituted for the more luxurious pine nuts if preferred.

25 g (1 oz) unsalted butter
1 large onion, peeled and very finely chopped
3 garlic cloves, peeled and crushed
50 g (2 oz) pine nuts
4–6 canned anchovy fillets, drained and pounded to a paste
175 ml (6 fl oz) double cream
120 ml (4 fl oz) cream or curd cheese
Maldon or sea salt
350 g (12 oz) fettucine
1 tablespoon olive oil
freshly ground black pepper
finely chopped fresh parsley

*Preparation time: 5 minutes
Cooking time: 25 minutes*

1. Melt the butter in a large saucepan, add the onion, cover and cook gently for 10 minutes until softened but not coloured. Add the garlic and pine nuts and cook for another 5 minutes.

2. Stir the pounded anchovy fillets into 2–3 tablespoons cream, then gradually stir in the rest of the cream and mix into the cheese. When quite smooth, stir into the onions in the pan and cook very gently for 10 minutes.

3. Meanwhile, bring a large pan of salted water to the boil, add the fettucine and boil for 7–8 minutes until just cooked but still with a slight 'bite'.

4. Drain well, then return to the pan with the oil, stirring until thoroughly coated. Tip the pasta into the cream sauce, mix thoroughly and season with black pepper and salt, if necessary. Transfer to a hot serving dish, sprinkle with parsley and serve at once.

COD STEAKS IN FRESH CORIANDER SAUCE

Cod is much underrated, often overcooked and swamped in a bland sauce. Yet its sweet, firm flesh lends itself to a partnership with strong flavours, and to a minimum of cooking. Watercress makes a good substitute for fresh coriander if the latter is unobtainable, and for a more economical dish you could make a white sauce, using half fish stock and half milk. Don't make it too thick, keep it really smooth and, for extra glossiness, whisk in a tablespoon of butter at the finish.

4 cod steaks, 175–225 g (6–8 oz) each
finely ground sea salt
freshly ground black pepper
100 g (4 oz) unsalted butter
½ onion, peeled and finely sliced
1 carrot, shredded
1 garlic clove, peeled and finely chopped
1 bay leaf
1 tablespoon dry Vermouth (optional)
120 ml (4 fl oz) fish stock
1 small bunch fresh coriander leaves, very finely chopped
120 ml (4 fl oz) double cream
1–2 tablespoons lemon juice
To garnish:
lime slices
Continental parsley sprigs

Preparation time: 10 minutes
Cooking time: 40 minutes
Oven: 190°C, 375°F, Gas Mark 5

1. Rinse the cod steaks in cold water, pat dry and season with salt and pepper.
2. Melt half the butter in a small pan, add the onion and carrot and sweat gently for 4–5 minutes. Add the garlic and cook for another 2 minutes.
3. Pour into a shallow ovenproof dish, add the bay leaf, then arrange the fish on top in a single layer. Sprinkle with Vermouth, if using, then with the fish stock. Cover with a butter paper (page 7) and cook in the preheated oven for 20–30 minutes until the fish just flakes easily when tested with a fork.
4. Remove the fish to a warmed serving plate and keep warm.
5. Strain the cooking juices into a clean pan and boil hard for 1–2 minutes to reduce.
6. Add half the remaining butter, the coriander leaves and the cream, and allow to bubble for 4–5 minutes until slightly thickened. Add the lemon juice, stir for a minute, then whisk in the last piece of butter, until smooth and glossy. Adjust the seasoning if necessary, then pour over the fish, garnish with lime slices and sprigs of Continental parsley and serve.

CIDER BAKED RED MULLET

Red mullet are the finest members of their family and have a natural affinity with fennel; they are often grilled on a bed of fennel stalks. Do not confuse them with the gurnard – regrettably sometimes passed off as mullet. Not only is the latter much brighter in colour – a sparkling scarlet – it is infinitely superior in taste. Grey mullet are another tribe altogether, good in their own right and much cheaper but, again, not so fine in flavour.

4 red mullet, cleaned and scaled, each about 350 g (12 oz)
2 tablespoons olive oil
1 large onion, peeled and finely chopped
2 large bulbs fresh fennel, leaves reserved
1–2 garlic cloves, peeled and crushed
300 ml (½ pint) dry cider
150 ml (¼ pint) cold water
3 tablespoons finely chopped fresh chervil or parsley
1 mace blade
finely ground sea salt
freshly ground black pepper
¼ teaspoon tomato purée
4–5 tablespoons double cream

Preparation time: 10 minutes
Cooking time: 50 minutes
Oven: 190°C, 375°F, Gas Mark 5

1. Rinse the mullet quickly in cold water.
2. Heat the oil in a large frying pan, add the onion and fry gently for 5 minutes. Meanwhile, slice the fennel very finely. Add to the pan together with the crushed garlic, stir-fry over a high heat for 2 minutes, then cover and cook gently for 10–15 minutes until the vegetables have softened.
3. Transfer the vegetables to a shallow ovenproof dish, spreading them in an even layer. Arrange the fish on top, then pour the cider and water over. Sprinkle over the chervil and bury the mace blade in the middle. Season with salt and a generous grinding of black pepper, then cover with a butter paper (page 7).
4. Bake in the preheated oven for 20–30 minutes until the fish flake easily. Remove carefully with a fish slice, then strain the liquid into a fresh pan. Make a bed of the vegetables on a serving dish, discarding the mace blade, and arrange the fish on top. Cover and keep warm in the turned off oven while finishing the sauce.
5. Reduce the liquid by hard boiling to about half its original quantity, then stir in the tomato purée. Stir for a minute, then pour in the cream. Allow to bubble for 2–3 minutes, then pour over the fish. Garnish with the reserved fennel leaves and serve immediately.

Cider baked red mullet; Cod steak in fresh coriander sauce

GRATINEED WHOLE PLAICE

*Except as a topping for fish pie, in England cheese
and fish are seldom combined, whereas in Italy it is a
favourite combination. Sole is the preferred fish in the
Italian kitchen, but cheese is also an excellent partner
for cod, halibut, turbot and brill or for plaice,
as in this delicious recipe.*

150 g (5 oz) unsalted butter
4 medium plaice, about 350 g (12 oz) each, skinned
finely ground sea salt
freshly ground black pepper
4 tablespoons lemon juice
4 tablespoons grated Parmesan cheese
finely chopped fresh parsley, to garnish

*Preparation time: 10 minutes
Cooking time: 15–20 minutes
Oven: 190°C, 375°F, Gas Mark 5*

1. Melt half the butter in a large shallow flameproof
casserole (or in a roasting tin standing over 2 rings or
burners). Add the fish and fry gently for 2–3 minutes
each side until lightly golden.
2. Sprinkle each fish with a little salt and pepper, then
dot with the remaining butter. Sprinkle 1 tablespoon
each of lemon juice and Parmesan over each one, then
cook in the preheated oven for 10–15 minutes until the
flesh flakes easily. Transfer to a serving platter and pour
the juices over.
3. Garnish with lots of parsley and serve immediately
with green salad.

BAKED COD STEAKS WITH MUSTARD SEEDS

Serves 6
6 cod steaks, each about 200–225 g (7–8 oz) in weight
1 tablespoon olive oil
2 tablespoons mustard seeds
175 g (6 oz) unsalted butter
2 tablespoons dry white wine
Maldon or sea salt
freshly ground black pepper
1–2 tablespoons Dijon mustard
3 tablespoons soured cream
finely chopped fresh parsley, to garnish

Preparation time: 5 minutes
Cooking time: 25–30 minutes
Oven: 190°C, 375°F, Gas Mark 5

1. Rinse the cod steaks in cold water and pat dry.
2. Put the oil in a small deep saucepan, add the mustard seeds and cook over a medium heat until they start popping and jumping about. Take off the heat immediately and drain.
3. Melt the butter in a large flame-proof dish into which the cod will fit neatly in one layer.
4. Add the steaks and fry until lightly golden on both sides, about 1–2 minutes each side. Sprinkle over the wine and the mustard seeds, season with salt and a good grinding of pepper, then cover with a butter paper.
5. Bake in the preheated oven for 20–25 minutes until the fish is just done – it should be very slightly underdone by the bone for perfect juiciness. Transfer the fish to a warmed serving platter.
6. Put the pan over a low heat, stir in 1 tablespoon of the mustard and the soured cream, whisking for 30 seconds. Taste and add the second tablespoon mustard if wished, then pour the sauce over the steaks. Sprinkle with parsley and serve immediately.

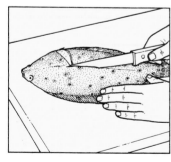
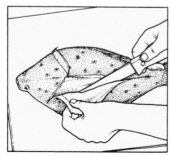

1. *Make a slit down the middle but do not cut through bone.*

2. *Cut round head. Slip knife underneath flesh to ease it away from bone.*

FRIED PLAICE WITH SESAME SEEDS

A marriage between the French and the Chinese, this adapts the cooking method of that classic dish, sole meunière, with a hint of the orient to add flavour to the plaice. Clarified butter is a must, otherwise it will burn.

Serves 6
3 large plaice, whole or filleted
Maldon or sea salt
freshly ground black pepper
3–4 tablespoons flour
12 spring onions, green tops only, shredded diagonally
1 tablespoon soy sauce
100 g (4 oz) clarified butter (page 18)
75 g (3 oz) unsalted butter
4 tablespoons sesame seeds
lemon wedges, to serve

Preparation time: 15–20 minutes
Cooking time: 5–6 minutes (excluding clarifying the butter)

1. To fillet the fish if you have bought them whole, using very sharp kitchen scissors, cut off the fins, leaving the heads and tails. Put the fish on a damp cloth to prevent it slipping, then make a slit with a knife down the middle from head to tail. Cut all round the head, then work down centre of the fish, pushing the knife under the flesh to free it from the bone. Work from the bone towards the outside edges, then cut the fillet off at the tail end. Repeat with the second fillet, turn over the fish and do the same on the second side. Remove spotted skin, keeping skin, bones, heads and tails for stock.
2. Rinse the fillets in cold water, pat dry and rub with a little salt and lots of pepper.[A]
3. Spread the flour on a flat surface and quickly dip the fillets in the flour, coating both sides lightly.
4. Before starting to cook, prepare a bed for the fish by arranging the spring onions to cover a serving dish. Sprinkle with the soy sauce.
5. Melt the clarified butter in a roasting pan (over 2 rings or burners if necessary). When just bubbling, add the fillets and fry for 2–3 minutes each side – by the time you have turned them, the first should be almost ready.
6. Transfer the fish to the serving dish or dishes, wipe out the pan, then melt the unsalted butter over a high heat. Add the sesame seeds and swirl in the bubbling butter for 10–20 seconds, then immediately pour over the fish. Serve at once, with lemon wedges.

[A] The fish may be filleted, rinsed and patted dry up to 3 hours in advance. Do not salt or pepper them, though, until ready to start cooking. Keep them chilled but bring to room temperature before seasoning.

Baked cod steak with mustard seeds; Fried plaice with sesame seeds

TUNA AND CAPER SOUFFLE

Although fresh tuna is not easily available in England, its canned brother is a useful bulwark of the storecupboard. Canned or fresh, the best part of the fish is the tummy (look for the word ventresca *on cans of Italian fish, indicating it is of the highest quality). Any good brand canned in olive oil will do for this recipe – the oil keeping this rather dry fish nicely succulent.*

Serves 4–6
40 g (1½ oz) unsalted butter, plus extra for greasing
4–5 tablespoons finely chopped fresh parsley
300 ml (½ pint) milk
1 bay leaf
3 tablespoons flour
3 tablespoons double cream
4 eggs (size 1), separated
freshly grated nutmeg
Maldon or sea salt
freshly ground black pepper
4 tablespoons capers, drained and finely chopped
2 × 175 g (6 oz) cans tuna fish, drained
1 egg white (size 1)

Preparation time: 15 minutes
Cooking time: 40–50 minutes
Oven: 190°C, 375°F, Gas Mark 5

1. Grease a 1.4 litre (2½ pint) soufflé dish liberally with butter, then sprinkle the parsley all over, turning the dish around to coat the sides well.
2. Put the milk in a pan with the bay leaf and bring just to the boil. Strain into a jug and reserve.
3. In a fresh pan, melt the 40 g (1½ oz) butter, then sift in the flour and stir to make a thick paste. Take off the heat and add the milk, a tablespoon at a time to begin with, until all the milk has been incorporated. Return to the heat and bring to the boil, stirring all the time, until thickening. Simmer on a low heat for 5 minutes.
4. Stir in the cream, then the egg yolks, beating briskly to mix in well. Take off the heat, season with nutmeg, salt and pepper, then fold in the capers and tuna fish.
5. Whisk the 5 egg whites until stiff peaks form, beat 2 tablespoons of the mixture into the fish to lighten, then fold the rest in quickly and lightly using a metal spoon. Pour into the prepared soufflé dish.
6. Bake in the preheated oven for 25–30 minutes until well puffed up and golden on the top. Serve immediately.

STIR-FRIED FILLETS WITH MUSHROOMS

One of the great advantages of the Chinese kitchen is the very short cooking time many recipes require, ideal for fish – keeping its nutrients and moistness intact. Here the oriental method marries with English ingredients, particularly walnut ketchup – a great favourite of the Victorians and now appearing on many supermarket shelves – to produce a quick and delicious supper dish.

Serves 4–6
450–750 g (1–1½ lb) fresh fillets of cod, haddock, halibut, or other firm white fish
Maldon or sea salt
5 tablespoons oil
150 ml (¼ pint) fish stock (page 7)
1 tablespoon dry sherry or brandy
1–2 tablespoons walnut ketchup
pinch or two of sugar
100 g (4 oz) button mushrooms, finely sliced
1 teaspoon arrowroot
freshly ground black pepper
To garnish:
lime slices
sprig of coriander

*Preparation time: 10 minutes, plus standing
Cooking time: 6–7 minutes*

1. Cut the fish into long thin strips, place on a shallow dish and sprinkle lightly with salt, then leave for 10–15 minutes.
2. Heat 2 tablespoons of the oil in a large frying pan or wok and when nearly smoking add the fish. Stir-fry for 2 minutes, then add the stock, sherry or brandy, ketchup, together with a good pinch of sugar. Stir to mix and bring to the boil.
3. Reduce the heat and simmer for 2–3 minutes.
4. Meanwhile heat the remaining oil in another pan, add the finely sliced mushrooms and stir for 30 seconds, then add to the fish pan.
5. Mix the arrowroot with about a tablespoon cold water and stir into the pan. Raise the heat slightly and let the liquid bubble for another minute until lightly thickened. Season with pepper and add a little more ketchup or sugar if necessary, then garnish. Serve at once with boiled egg noodles or rice combined with petit pois.

When herbs are in abundance during the summer, it's a good idea to freeze some sprigs for winter cooking. Open freeze, then pack 2-3 sprigs in small bags or foil. They could also be chopped before freezing.

SALT COD FRITTERS

In Greece and the Levant these fritters served with a garlicky sauce are a favourite delicacy.

Serves 4–6
750 g (1¾ lb) salt cod
120 g (4 oz) flour
¼ teaspoon Maldon or sea salt
freshly ground white pepper
olive oil for deep frying
generous 150 ml (¼ pint) warm water
1 egg white (size 1)
2–4 garlic cloves, peeled and crushed
175 g (6 fl oz) thick mayonnaise
4 tablespoons finely chopped fresh parsley
pinch cayenne pepper
parsley sprig, to garnish
lemon wedges, to serve

*Preparation time: 15 minutes, plus soaking overnight
Cooking time: 5–15 minutes*

1. Soak the salt cod in a large bucket of cold water for 24 hours, changing the water every 2 hours when practical.
2. One hour before the end of the soaking time, make the batter. Sift the flour, salt and pepper into a large bowl, dribble over 1 tablespoon of the oil and the warm water. Whisk thoroughly until quite smooth, then leave to stand for 1 hour. Do not chill.
3. Drain the fish and peel away the skin. Cut the fish into large cubes, about 7.5 cm (1½ inches) across and remove as many large bones as possible. Pat dry.
4. Just before cooking, whisk the egg white until softly stiff, beat the batter quickly, then fold the egg into the batter.
5. Heat a good 5 cm (2 inches) of olive oil in a large pan until nearly smoking. Dip a few pieces of fish in the batter and carefully drop into the pan. Fry over a fairly high heat for about 4–5 minutes until golden and puffed up. Drain on paper towels and keep warm while cooking the rest.
6. Mix the garlic into the mayonnaise, then stir in the parsley and a good pinch of cayenne pepper. Garnish and serve the fritters at once with the mayonnaise and lots of lemon wedges.

Stir-fried fillets with mushrooms; Salt cod fritters

FRIED HERRINGS IN OATMEAL

Serves 6
6 large herrings, filleted
finely ground sea salt
freshly ground black pepper
75 g (3 oz) medium oatmeal
generous pinch ground nutmeg
100 g (4 oz) butter
<u>To serve:</u>
finely chopped fresh parsley
lemon wedges
thinly sliced brown bread and butter

Preparation time: 5 minutes
Cooking time: 10–15 minutes

1. Rinse the herrings and thoroughly pat dry with paper towels. Season generously on both sides with salt and pepper.
2. Mix the oatmeal with the nutmeg then turn the fillets in the mixture. Make sure that the herrings are coated thickly and evenly on both sides with the mixture.
3. Melt the butter in a large frying pan (or two if necessary). When just sizzling, add the fish and cook over a medium heat for about 5–7 minutes each side until crisp and cooked through.
4. Drain the herrings and serve at once, sprinkled with the finely chopped parsley and accompanied by lemon wedges and plenty of thinly sliced brown bread and butter.

SUMMER FISH

GRILLED RAINBOW TROUT WITH GROUND ALMOND PASTE

Serves 6
6 small rainbow trout, about 275 g (10 oz) in weight each, cleaned but heads and tails left on
225 g (8 oz) ground almonds
4–6 tablespoons olive oil
Maldon or sea salt
freshly ground black pepper
1 tablespoon lemon juice
2 tablespoons finely chopped fresh parsley
sprigs of fresh chervil, to garnish

Preparation time: 15 minutes
Cooking time: 15–20 minutes

1. Rinse the trout quickly in cold water and pat dry with paper towels.
2. Put the ground almonds in a bowl, add 4 tablespoons oil, season well with salt and pepper, and add the lemon juice and parsley. The paste should be thin enough to coat the fish without falling off. If too thick add extra oil.
3. Smear the paste over each fish. Grill over a very hot barbecue (or under a hot grill) for 7–10 minutes each side until the fish is done and the skin beautifully crisp and deep golden. Garnish and serve at once.

BARBECUED RED MULLET WITH CORIANDER SEEDS AND GARLIC

Serves 6
6 small red mullet, cleaned, livers not removed
3 tablespoons olive oil
2 tablespoons coriander seeds, lightly crushed
3–4 garlic cloves, peeled and finely chopped
Maldon or sea salt
freshly ground white pepper
To garnish:
lemon slices
bay leaves

Preparation time: 5 minutes
Cooking time: 15–20 minutes

1. Rinse the mullet quickly and pat dry. Brush with 1 tablespoon of the oil and leave for 5 minutes.
2. Heat the remaining oil in a frying pan, add the coriander seeds and garlic and fry for 2 minutes.
3. Brush the fish with some of this mixture, sprinkle with salt and pepper, and cook over a preheated hot barbecue (or under a hot grill) for 4–5 minutes. Turn and brush with the rest of the oil, then grill for 4–5 minutes until crisp. Garnish and serve immediately.

FILLETS OF SOLE EN PAPILLOTE WITH TARRAGON, WINE AND BUTTER

Serves 6
12 large sole fillets, about 1.25 kg (2¾ lb) total weight
150 g (5 oz) unsalted butter, cut into 6 pieces
6 sprigs fresh tarragon
150 ml (¼ pint) dry white wine
3–4 tablespoons olive oil
6 tablespoons day-old breadcrumbs
Maldon salt
freshly ground black pepper

Preparation time: 10 minutes
Cooking time: 15 minutes

1. If you wish, slice the fillets into long thin strips.
2. Cut 6 pieces of foil into 20 cm (8 inch) squares. Use the pieces of butter to grease each one, then divide the sole between the packets. Dot with the remaining pieces of butter, put a sprig of tarragon on each one then sprinkle the wine over.
3. Heat the oil in a frying pan, add the breadcrumbs and stir-fry for 1–2 minutes, adding more oil if necessary, until the crumbs are crisp. Scatter over the sole, season with salt and pepper and seal the parcels tightly.
4. Cook the parcels over a very hot barbecue for 8–10 minutes, then serve at once in the packets. Plenty of French bread and a chilled dry wine are the only accompaniments needed.

Grilled rainbow trout with ground almond paste; Barbecued red mullet with coriander seeds and garlic

SMOKED HADDOCK SALAD WITH WATERCRESS MAYONNAISE

Smoked haddock is a very versatile fish, as good cold as it is hot. Watercress supplies piquancy to the dressing, but for an exotic touch you could use a small bunch of fresh coriander leaves instead, in which case add a few crushed coriander seeds to the milk when poaching the fish.

Serves 6
1 kg (2 lb) smoked haddock
600 ml (1 pint) milk
1 small onion, peeled but left whole
2 cloves
large bunch of watercress, washed and stems discarded
225 ml (8 fl oz) good mayonnaise
2 tablespoons plain unsweetened yogurt
1 teaspoon paprika
freshly ground black pepper
2 medium bulbs fennel, finely shredded, leaves reserved for garnish
Maldon or sea salt (optional)
2 eggs, hard-boiled

Preparation time: 10 minutes
Cooking time: 20–25 minutes

1. Rinse the haddock, put in a shallow dish and cover with boiling water. Leave for 2 minutes, then drain and refresh in cold water.
2. Put into a large pan, pour in the milk and add water until the fish is just covered. Add the onion, studded with the cloves, and bring to the boil. Simmer for 20–25 minutes.
3. Drain the fish (reserving the milk for soup). Remove the skin and as many bones as possible, then flake into bite-sized pieces.
4. Take half the watercress and either chop finely in a food processor, or chop by hand then pound lightly in a pestle and mortar. Mix the chopped watercress into the mayonnaise and stir in the yogurt, paprika and some freshly ground black pepper.
5. Mix the haddock into the mayonnaise, then fold in the shredded fennel.[A]
6. Taste the mixture, adding a little salt if necessary, then pile into a serving dish.
7. Arrange the remaining watercress on the fish, then halve the boiled eggs and remove the yolks. Crumble lightly with a fork and sprinkle over the fish. Serve at room temperature with boiled rice or pasta, lightly dressed with olive oil. Garnish with fennel leaves.

[A] The fish mixture may be prepared in advance, covered and kept for up to 4 hours. Bring to room temperature before serving.

MARINATED HERRING AND NEW POTATO SALAD

If you grow fennel you will usually be able to find a few sprigs even on the coldest winter days. Otherwise, buy a bulb generously endowed with feathery leaves and chop them off for the salad, and use the bulb for soup or to braise. Or you could add it to the salad, to replace some of the potatoes.

Serves 6
1 tablespoon Maldon or sea salt
2 tablespoons olive oil
1 tablespoon caster sugar
1 teaspoon white peppercorns, crushed in a pestle and mortar
1 tablespoon finely chopped fresh tarragon
½ teaspoon dill seeds, lightly crushed
2 large herrings, cleaned and boned, heads removed
450 g (1 lb) small new potatoes, scrubbed
175 ml (6 fl oz) good mayonnaise
1–2 teaspoons Dijon mustard
To garnish:
sprig of fresh tarragon
1 tablespoon fresh dill seed

Preparation time: 25 minutes, plus marinating
Cooking time: 10 minutes

1. Mix the salt, oil, sugar, peppercorns, tarragon and dill seeds together and spread a layer over the bottom of a shallow dish into which the herrings will fit snugly (so that they are lying flat).
2. Put one of the fish, skin side down, into the dish and spread more of the paste all over the flesh. Cover with the second fish, skin side up this time, then spread the remaining mixture over the skin. Cover the dish with foil and weight down (use a plate with a couple of cans on top). Chill for a minimum of 12 hours, up to 4 days if possible.
3. About 30 minutes before serving, boil the potatoes in lightly salted water for 8–10 minutes until done, checking after 5–6 minutes if they are really small. Drain thoroughly and cut in half if necessary. Set them aside to cool slightly.
4. Cut the fish on the diagonal into thin slices, in the same way as slicing smoked salmon. Mix into the cooled potatoes.
5. Mix the mayonnaise with mustard to taste, then toss the fish and potatoes in the dressing.
6. Pile the fish and potato salad into a serving bowl and sprinkle with the fresh tarragon and dill seeds. Serve at once.

LEFT TO RIGHT: *Smoked haddock salad with watercress mayonnaise; Marinated herring and new potato salad*

HOT KIPPER AND MUSHROOM
SALAD

An unusual hot salad, simple but delicious – and ideal for shivery summer days. Don't be tempted to substitute kipper fillets for this dish – they do not have the same fullness of flavour.

Serves 6
3 large kippers
225 g (8 oz) button mushrooms, wiped clean
5–7 tablespoons olive oil
3–4 tablespoons plain unsweetened yogurt
2–3 tablespoons lemon juice
freshly ground allspice
freshly ground black pepper
3 tablespoons finely chopped fresh parsley
6 large lettuce leaves, washed and drained
3 spring onions, green tops only, shredded diagonally
thinly sliced brown bread and butter, to serve

Preparation time: 20 minutes
Cooking time: 12 minutes

1. Put the kippers, heads down, into a large jug. Fill with boiling water, right up to the top, and press down on the fish tails if necessary to immerse them completely. Cover the jug and leave for 10 minutes.
2. Slice the mushrooms very thinly. Heat 5 tablespoons oil in a large frying pan.
3. Add the mushrooms to the pan and stir-fry for just 1 minute so that they are still quite crunchy. Quickly tip into a large, warmed bowl. If they seem a little dry, add a little extra oil.
4. Pour some boiling water into a saucepan over which the bowl will sit comfortably. Keep the water at a very gentle simmer.
5. Drain the kippers, and working as quickly as possible, cut off the heads and tails, then remove the large back bone and as many small bones as you can. Flake the fish and add to the mushrooms.
6. Mix well, then add the yogurt and a little lemon juice. Grind in a generous amount of allspice and some black pepper and stir in the parsley. Taste, adding more yogurt or lemon as you wish.
7. Arrange the lettuce leaves on individual plates. Spoon the fish mixture on top and sprinkle over the spring onion tops. Serve at once with brown bread and butter.

MONKFISH AND AVOCADO SALAD

One of the most perfect summer combinations, both for appearance and flavour. Nasturtium leaves and flowers are not essential but do provide a vivid finishing touch. They grow well – even in a pot on a window sill.

Serves 6
1.25–1.5 kg (2½–3 lb) tailpiece monkfish
6 tablespoons olive oil
Maldon or sea salt
freshly ground black pepper
2 garlic cloves, peeled and finely chopped
2 tablespoons finely chopped fresh basil
1 beef tomato, skinned, seeded and drained
225 ml (8 fl oz) mayonnaise
2–3 drops Tabasco, or to taste
3 nasturtium leaves (optional)
3 large avocados
1–2 tablespoons lemon juice
6 nasturtium flowers or carnation petals

*Preparation time: 30 minutes, plus marinating
Cooking time: 5–8 minutes*

1. Bone the fish (page 73) and cut into 2 triangular fillets. Put into a shallow dish and cover with the oil. Sprinkle over salt and pepper, the garlic cloves and half the chopped basil. Leave for 30 minutes, turning once.
2. Put the fish on a foil-lined grill rack and cook under a very hot grill for 2½–4 minutes each side depending on the thickness of the fish. It should be firm to the touch so that it will slice easily with a sharp knife, but not overcooked. Remove from the grill and leave to cool.[A]
3. Chop the tomato very finely, then fold into the mayonnaise with the remaining basil. Add the Tabasco and the chopped nasturtium leaves, if using.[A]
4. Just before serving, cut the avocados in half, remove the stones, then quickly peel and thinly slice. Arrange on plates, and drizzle over a little lemon juice.
5. Slice the fish into 3 long fillets, then thinly slice them diagonally and arrange on top of the avocado.
6. Taste the mayonnaise, adding a little salt and pepper if necessary, then put a couple of spoonfuls on each plate, over the fish and the avocado. Garnish and serve.

[A] The fish may be cooked up to 1 hour in advance and left to cool, covered. The mayonnaise may be made up to 1 hour ahead, covered and kept chilled.

DRESSED CRAB SALAD

Rich, sweet and filling, crab is a luxurious seafood at a sensible price. Some find its preparation daunting, yet all that is required is patience, a shellpick or fine skewer – and time. And if you should be lucky enough to be offered live crabs, they are simple to cook. Very salt water is essential, about 175 g (6 oz) salt to 2–2.5 litres (3½–4 pints) water or, if you are near the sea, add enough salt to seawater to make an egg float in it. Bring to the boil in a very large pan, add the crab, cover tightly and simmer for 15 minutes for the first 450 g (1 lb), 10 minutes each 450 g (1 lb) thereafter. Cool on its back to keep it moist.

Serves 6
2 large boiled crabs, about 1–1.25 kg (2–2½ lb) each
2 egg yolks
Maldon or sea salt
freshly ground black pepper
300 ml (½ pint) olive oil
1 large lemon
½–1 teaspoon Dijon mustard
freshly ground white pepper
pinch of cayenne pepper
1 teaspoon finely chopped fresh tarragon
½ teaspoon capers
1 teaspoon snipped chives
To garnish:
salad burnet leaves
1 tablespoon finely chopped chives
lemon rind, finely grated
paprika

Preparation time: 1½–2 hours
Cooking time: 5 minutes

1. Have ready 2 bowls, a clear working surface, a shell-pick or long skewer, a teaspoon, a sterilized hammer and a large, heavy-bladed knife.
2. Prepare each crab in the same way. Lay each crab on its back, break off the large claws and the legs and set aside. Push the tip of the knife under the pointed tail flap and prise up. It will come away with the chest meat, leaving the main body behind. Reserve the chest and start on the main shell.
3. Remove the small, translucent crinkled bag near the mouth (this is the stomach) and discard. Then snap off the mouth and discard that too, together with any broken pieces of white membrane or gills which may have come loose from the chest.
4. Spoon out all the soft, creamy, yellowish-brown meat and put into one of the bowls. Any soft pale pink flesh on the side of the shell should also be scooped out and added to the bowl. Scrub the shell under cold water, then tap sharply along the curved line that runs right round the shell, discarding the pieces that you break off. You now have a neat container for the dressed crab. Boil the shells for 5 minutes and leave to drain.

5. Crack the claws from the crabs, extracting the large pieces of white flesh, then dig with the skewer if necessary to remove the tips. Put the flesh into the second bowl. Break the smaller legs at the joints and pull out the fibrous meat adding to the second bowl. (Keep the claws and legs for making stock, adding the crushed shell once you've had the salad.)
6. Now tackle the chest pieces, first removing and discarding the poisonous white gills (dead man's fingers) then scooping out any yellowish meat and adding to the first bowl. If necessary, break the chest into 2–3 pieces, and prise out all the white fibrous flesh, being careful not to add any of the thin transparent membranes – they are not poisonous but can stick in the throat. Mash the white meat lightly together, flaking any large pieces, then put aside. Mash and flake the brownish-yellow meat in the first bowl in the same way.
7. Whisk the egg yolks in another bowl with a good pinch of salt and black pepper. Whisk in a few drops of oil, mix in thoroughly, then add a few more drops of oil, gradually working up to a thin stream whisking vigorously all the time so that the oil is absorbed. Stop when you have added about two-thirds of the oil, or if the mixture is becoming too thick to absorb more easily.
8. Grate off about 1 tablespoon of lemon rind, then cut the lemon in half and squeeze 1 tablespoon of juice into the mayonnaise. Add the rind and stir in well. Now add the rest of the oil, whisking continuously. When the mayonnaise is thick and shiny, beat in another ½–1 tablespoon lemon juice, and taste, adding a little extra if it needs sharpening further. Transfer 5–6 tablespoons to a separate smaller bowl.
9. Mix the white crab meat with about two-thirds of the mayonnaise, adding more if it seems a little dry – it should be creamy but not swimming in mayonnaise.[A]
10. Mix the mayonnaise in the smaller bowl with the mustard to taste, then add a little freshly ground white pepper, the cayenne, finely chopped tarragon, capers and chives and blend together thoroughly.
11. Mix the brown meat with 3 tablespoons of the mustardy mayonnaise, again adding a little more if necessary – the mixture should taste piquant, and be smooth and creamy.[A]
12. Arrange the white flesh in the crab shells, at both ends, then pile the brown meat in the middle and arrange a line of salad burnet leaves along the 'joins'.
13. Sprinkle the middle with chopped chives, grated lemon rind and a pinch of paprika. Serve with a tossed green salad.

[A] The separate bowls of crab flesh can be prepared up to 2 hours in advance and covered, kept chilled. Give them a quick stir before piling into the shells.

Dressed crab salad; Monkfish and avocado salad

PLAICE FILLET AND BACON SALAD

Serves 6
750 g–1 kg (1–2 lb) plaice fillets, skinned
1.2 litres (2 pints) fish stock (page 7)
2 strands saffron
6 streaky bacon rashers, rinds removed
6 lettuce hearts
2–3 teaspoons cider vinegar
Maldon or sea salt
freshly ground white pepper
2 tablespoons snipped chives
2–3 drops Anisette or Pernod (optional)
50 g (2 oz) red lumpfish roe
4 whole chives, to garnish

Preparation time: 10 minutes
Cooking time: 15 minutes

1. Cut the fillets into long thin strips and set aside.
2. Bring the fish stock to the boil in a large pan, turn the heat low so the liquid is barely simmering, then add the fish and poach for 2–3 minutes until just cooked.[A] Take care not to overcook or it will disintegrate. Drain, reserving the liquid, and put the fish in a covered bowl, so that it doesn't cool too quickly.
3. Strain the stock through a fine muslin (or a coffee filter) and return to the rinsed-out pan. Crumble the saffron strands, put in a small bowl and pour over 2 tablespoons of the stock. Stir then leave for 4–5 minutes until the colour runs. Meanwhile boil the remaining stock hard until reduced to a scant 400 ml (14 fl oz).[A]
4. While the stock is boiling grill the bacon under a very hot grill until crisp. Chop into small dice.
5. Strain the saffron liquid into the stock. Take off the heat and plunge the pan into a bowl of very cold water (add a few ice cubes). Leave while arranging the salad.
6. Toss the bacon and the plaice strips together. Arrange the lettuce heart leaves on individual serving plates. Divide the plaice and bacon between the plates.
7. Stir a little cider vinegar into the cooled stock. Add a touch of salt and a generous grinding of white pepper – then taste to see if it needs a little more vinegar. The dressing should have a 'bite' without being too sharp.
8. Sprinkle some chives over each salad and add a few drops of Anisette to the dressing if wished. Spoon 3–3½ tablespoons dressing over the salads.
9. Add a spoonful of lumpfish roe to each plate. Garnish and serve at once.

[A] The fish may be poached up to 3 hours in advance, in which case it should only be cooked just until firm and opaque. Keep, covered, in a colander or steamer, then steam for 1 minute to reheat, just before assembling the salad. The stock can also be strained and reduced up to 3 hours in advance. Bring it quickly to simmering point just before making the salad, then stir in the saffron liquid.

MEDITERRANEAN PRAWN AND BROCCOLI SALAD

Serves 6
18 Mediterranean prawns
450–750 g (1–1½ lb) young fresh broccoli, or 450 g (1 lb) frozen broccoli, thawed
Maldon or sea salt
1 large avocado
3 spring onions, bulbs finely sliced, green tops cut into fine rings
2 tablespoons finely chopped fresh parsley
freshly ground black pepper
For the dressing:
1 small garlic clove, peeled and finely chopped
¼ teaspoon grated fresh ginger root
6 tablespoons olive oil
2–3 tablespoons lemon juice

Preparation time: 30 minutes
Cooking time: about 5 minutes

1. Shell the prawns, keeping the heads and shells for stock (page 7).[A]
2. Cut the broccoli into florets with about 5 cm (2 inches) of stem left on. Rinse in cold water.
3. Bring a large pan of lightly salted water to the boil, add the broccoli and cook for 3–5 minutes until just tender, but still with a bite. Drain, refresh under cold running water and leave to cool in the colander while making the dressing.
4. Mix the garlic, salt, a good grinding of black pepper and the grated ginger in a small bowl or jug. Briskly stir in the oil, then 2 tablespoons lemon juice, mixing well. Taste, adding extra lemon juice if necessary – the dressing should be lemony but not sharp.
5. Pour 3 tablespoons dressing into a bowl, add the broccoli florets (which should still be slightly warm) and toss until the dressing is completely absorbed.[A]
6. Just before serving, quickly cut the avocado in half, remove the stone, then peel back the skin from each half. Cut the flesh into 18 slices. Arrange 3 slices on each plate, then lay 3 prawns on top and the broccoli around the outside edge.
7. Scatter over the spring onions, then the parsley and grind some black pepper on top. Pour a little dressing over the salad and serve at once, with a lightly chilled, crisp dry white wine.

[A] The prawns may be prepared up to 3 hours in advance, wrapped in cling film and kept in a cool place, preferably not the refrigerator. The 'dressed' broccoli can be prepared, covered and kept in its bowl for up to 3 hours. Do not chill.

Plaice fillet and bacon salad; Mediterranean prawn and broccoli salad

SOY MARINATED PLAICE

Fish responds well to marinades, absorbing the new flavours as its own increases. This marinade is particularly good for a mild-tasting fish, especially if it has been frozen.

Serves 6
6 medium plaice, about 350 g (12 oz) each, spotted skin removed
4 tablespoons soy sauce
3 tablespoons dry sherry
4 tablespoons peanut oil
2 tablespoons fresh lime juice
3 spring onions, green tops only, cut into very fine rings
2 garlic cloves, peeled and very finely chopped
Maldon or sea salt (optional)
freshly ground black pepper

Preparation time: 10 minutes, plus marinating
Cooking time: 10–15 minutes

1. Rinse the fish and lightly pat dry. Lay in one layer in a large shallow dish.
2. Mix the soy sauce, sherry, oil, and lime juice together and pour over the fish. Cover and leave at room temperature for 1 hour, turning 2–3 times.[A]
3. Remove the fish from the marinade and cook under a preheated very hot grill or over a hot barbecue for 5–7 minutes each side, brushing occasionally with a little marinade.
4. Put the rest of the marinade into a small heavy saucepan and bring to the boil either on the stove or over the barbecue. Add the spring onions and garlic and boil for 1 minute.
5. Transfer the fish to individual plates, spoon over some of the juices, onions and garlic and serve immediately, sprinkled with a little salt, if wished, and a good grinding of black pepper.

[A] The fish may be marinated for up to 6 hours. Keep it covered and chilled and bring to room temperature before cooking.

MONKFISH KEBABS WITH CUMIN AND MINT

Cumin is a taste that once acquired is never lost. Combined with the sweetness of mint, it gives monkfish an exotic flavour.

Serves 6
1.5 kg (3 lb) tailpiece monkfish, skinned and filleted (page 73)
120 ml (4 fl oz) olive oil
1 tablespoon lemon juice
1 tablespoon cumin seeds, lightly crushed
2 tablespoons finely chopped fresh mint, lightly pounded, or 1 tablespoon dried mint
Maldon or sea salt
freshly ground black pepper
150 ml (5 fl oz) plain unsweetened yogurt, chilled, to serve

Preparation time: 10 minutes, plus marinating
Cooking time: 5 minutes

1. Cut the monkfish into bite-sized cubes and put into a large shallow dish. Combine the oil, lemon juice, cumin seeds and mint. Season with salt and a fair amount of black pepper then pour over the fish. Stir to coat, then leave at room temperature for 1 hour.[A]
2. Thread the fish on to 6 skewers and grill over a very hot barbecue for 4–5 minutes, turning every minute until just done, brushing frequently with the marinade.
3. Serve immediately, providing the yogurt as a dip, with pitta or crusty bread.

[A] May be prepared up to 24 hours in advance and kept chilled. Bring to room temperature before cooking.

SALMON KEBABS WITH VERMOUTH

Tail pieces of salmon can often be bought cheaply from the fishmonger and are ideal for a recipe such as this. You could also use cod, haddock or any firm white fish.

Serves 4–6
1 kg (2 lb) tailpiece fresh salmon, skinned
175 g (6 oz) unsalted butter, softened
5 tablespoons dry Vermouth
Maldon or sea salt
freshly ground black pepper
50 g (2 oz) day-old breadcrumbs
1 tablespoon olive oil
25 g (1 oz) sesame seeds
To garnish:
lime slices
fennel leaves

Preparation time: 25 minutes
Cooking time: 5–8 minutes

1. Remove centre bone from salmon, as if filleting monkfish (page 73), then cut into 25 mm (1 inch) cubes.
2. Beat the butter with the Vermouth, a little salt and lots of black pepper, whisking to make a smooth paste.
3. Thread the fish cubes on to 4–6 thin skewers, then smear all over with the butter paste.
4. Put the breadcrumbs on a flat plate or work surface, and press the fish lightly into them to coat all over.
5. Remove the grill rack, place the skewers in the grill pan and cook under a preheated, very hot grill for 5–7 minutes, turning every minute, until the fish is just done. Transfer the skewers to individual serving plates.
6. Pour any cooking juices from the grill pan into a small saucepan, add the oil and heat. Stir in the sesame seeds, cook for a minute until golden, then pour over the kebabs. Garnish, then serve at once.

PARSLEYED HALIBUT KEBABS

For a more formal occasion, adapt this recipe to use whole steaks of halibut.

Serves 6
1 kg (2 lb) halibut fillet, skinned and cut into 25 mm (1 inch) cubes
175 g (6 oz) butter, softened
¼ teaspoon fennel seeds, finely ground
1 teaspoon Anisette or Pernod
1 large bunch parsley, stems discarded
Maldon salt
freshly ground black pepper
lemon wedges, to serve (optional)

Preparation time: 25 minutes
Cooking time: 5 minutes

1. Pat the fish quite dry with paper towels and reserve.
2. Whisk the butter with the fennel seeds and Anisette. Thread the fish on to 6 skewers and spread with the butter paste.
3. Chop the parsley very finely, in a food processor if available. Spread all over a flat plate or work surface, and roll the skewers in it until completely covered. Remove the rack from the grill tray and place the skewers on it.
4. Cook the fish under a preheated very hot grill for 5 minutes, turning every minute, until the fish is done and the parsley crisp and dark green. Serve at once, sprinkled with salt and pepper, accompanied by lemon wedges if wished.

CLOCKWISE FROM BOTTOM: *Salmon kebabs with vermouth; Parsleyed halibut kebabs; Monkfish kebabs with cumin and mint*

PAPRIKA COD SALAD

Serves 6
1 kg (2 lb) cod fillet, in not more than 2 large pieces
Maldon or sea salt
freshly ground black pepper
3 parsley sprigs
1 bay leaf
1 × 5 cm (2 inch) piece lemon rind
6 white peppercorns, lightly crushed
1 mace blade
150 ml (¼ pint) dry white wine
1 litre (1¾ pints) cold water
2 large red peppers
105–175 ml (5–6 fl oz) olive oil
1–2 garlic cloves, peeled and finely chopped
2 tablespoons sweet paprika
½ large Spanish onion, peeled and very finely chopped
2–3 tablespoons lemon juice
3 tablespoons finely chopped fresh parsley

Preparation time: 20 minutes, plus cooling
Cooking time: 45–50 minutes

1. Rinse the cod in cold water. Put in a shallow dish and sprinkle with a little salt and black pepper, then leave while making the bouillon.
2. Put the parsley, bay leaf, lemon rind, peppercorns, mace blade and wine into a large pan with the water. Bring slowly to the boil, then simmer gently for 30 minutes. Strain, then leave to cool.
3. While the bouillon is cooling, cut the peppers in half, remove the seeds and press the halves to flatten slightly if they are very curved. Place under a very hot grill, or over a gas flame until blackened. Remove from the heat and wrap in a damp tea-towel, then leave for 10 minutes.
4. Place the fish in one layer in a large frying pan or roasting pan. Pour over enough cool bouillon just to cover, bring slowly to the boil, then simmer on the lowest possible heat – the water should barely quiver – for about 10–15 minutes until the fish is firm to the touch and opaque. It should be almost slightly undercooked in the middle.
5. Meanwhile, peel the charred skin off the peppers, running any pieces that may have blackened right through to the flesh, under cold water and rubbing off all charred traces. Slice the peppers lengthways into thin strips, then place at one end of a long shallow serving dish, and dribble 50 ml (2 fl oz) oil over them.
6. Drain the cooked fish and cut into slices across the fillet. Place the slices in the dish with the peppers, keeping them slightly separate.
7. Mix the remaining oil with half the garlic cloves and the paprika, then pour over the fish, making sure the entire surface gets a small drizzling of oil. You may not need all the oil. Leave until barely warm to the touch.
8. Turn the fish over, pour on a little more oil, then spread the slices all over the dish, arranging the pepper strips on top – in a criss-cross pattern if you like. Scatter on the remaining chopped garlic and the onion, then pour on any leftover oil, and lemon juice to taste. Sprinkle with parsley and serve with crusty bread.

MACKEREL EN PAPILLOTE WITH GOOSEBERRIES AND NUTS

Serves 6
6 small mackerel, about 275–350 g (10–12 oz) each,
cleaned but heads and tails left on
Maldon or sea salt
freshly ground white pepper
275 g (10 oz) gooseberries, topped and tailed
75 g (3 oz) unsalted butter
½ teaspoon sugar (optional)
1 teaspoon lemon juice
75 g (3 oz) hazelnuts, finely chopped
¼ teaspoon green peppercorns, drained if in brine,
lightly crushed
6 tablespoons dry white wine or cider
sprigs of coriander, to garnish

Preparation time: 20 minutes
Cooking time: 35–45 minutes

1. Rinse the mackerel, rubbing any stubborn traces of blood with a little salt. Rub salt and pepper all over the fish and set aside.
2. To make the stuffing, put the gooseberries into a small pan, and add enough cold water to just cover. Bring to the boil, then simmer gently for 10–20 minutes until soft and pulpy and most of the liquid has been absorbed.
3. Stir in 25 g (1 oz) butter, and cook for a further 2 minutes, then taste and add sugar if necessary. Stir in the lemon juice, nuts and peppercorns.[A]
4. Cut out 6 pieces of foil, each large enough to enclose the fish with a good edge left to seal the parcels. Grease all over with the remaining butter.
5. Stuff each fish, pushing the mixture through the belly cavity. Put each fish on a piece of foil. Sprinkle a tablespoon of wine or cider over each, grind over some white pepper, then seal the parcels tightly.
6. Cook over a preheated hot barbecue or in a moderate oven for 20–25 minutes. Open the parcels, garnish and serve with crusty bread and a tomato salad.

[A] The fish may be prepared, and the stuffing cooked, up to 3 hours in advance, covered and kept cool until ready to cook. On a very hot day, chill the fish and bring to room temperature before stuffing.

Mackerel en papillote with gooseberries and nuts;
Paprika cod salad

CLASSIC FISH

WHOLE SEA BASS IN ASPIC

Serves 8

1 sea bass, 2 kg (4½ lb) cleaned, scaled, spine removed
(it's slightly poisonous) but head and tail left on
1 tablespoon finely chopped fresh tarragon
2 tablespoons chopped celery leaves
300 ml (½ pint) dry white wine
6 white peppercorns
freshly grated nutmeg
1 carrot, sliced
1 large onion, peeled and finely sliced
3–4 parsley sprigs
1 × 5 cm (2 inch) piece lemon rind
Maldon or sea salt
1 celery stalk, sliced diagonally
900 ml (1½ pints) water, plus 3 tablespoons cold water
1 tablespoon Madeira or dry sherry
2 tablespoons powdered gelatine
1 small cucumber
3–4 tomatoes, blanched, skinned and very finely
chopped, excess juice drained
1 tablespoon olive oil
1 tablespoon lemon juice
freshly ground black pepper
3–4 fresh tarragon sprigs
lemon slices and stuffed olive (optional), to garnish

*Preparation time: 1 hour, plus marinating, cooling and
setting
Cooking time: 1¼ hours*

1. Lay the fish in a shallow dish, sprinkle over the tarragon and celery leaves, then pour on the wine. Add the peppercorns and a good sprinkling of nutmeg then cover and leave to marinate for 3 hours, turning the fish carefully from time to time.[A]
2. Remove the fish and pour the marinade into a fish kettle or roasting pan. Add the carrot, onion, parsley sprigs, lemon rind, a pinch of salt and the celery. Pour in the 900 ml (1½ pints) cold water and bring to the boil. Turn the heat low and simmer for 30 minutes, then remove from the heat and allow to cool.
3. Carefully transfer the fish to the kettle or pan. Bring the liquid slowly to the boil, then allow to boil fairly vigorously for 1 minute. Take the kettle or pan off the heat and leave the fish to cool in the cooking liquid – it

will cook as it cools, giving a succulent result.[A]
4. Once the fish has cooked, transfer to a large dish, again taking care that it does not break. Strain the stock into a clean saucepan and quickly bring to the boil. Skim the stock then boil gently until reduced to 600 ml (1 pint). Cool for 10–15 minutes then skim any fat off the surface with paper towels. Stir in the Madeira or sherry.
5. Sprinkle the gelatine over the 3 tablespoons water in a small bowl, then stand it in a pan of simmering water until dissolved. Let the gelatine mixture cool to the same temperature as the stock.
6. Meanwhile, skin the fish on both sides, leaving the head and tail on, then transfer to a long serving platter.
7. Whisk the gelatine thoroughly into the stock, then leave until beginning to set – it should have the consistency of egg whites.
8. Cut a quarter of the cucumber into thin slices. Dice the rest, discarding the seeds. Combine the diced cucumber and chopped tomatoes in a bowl, then stir in the oil and lemon juice and season with salt and pepper.
9. Dip the tarragon sprigs into the setting aspic and arrange down the body of the fish. Dip the cucumber slices in aspic and arrange some in a 'collar' at the head end, and some at the tail end. Leave until set.
10. If the aspic has set too much, liquify it slightly by warming it gently over a pan of simmering water. Pour a thin layer over the entire fish and leave until set, then repeat the process, this time pouring all the aspic over. Don't worry if any aspic runs on to the platter.
11. When the aspic has set, dip a sharp thin-bladed knife into cold water, then cut through the aspic right around the fish. Scrape the aspic off the platter and chop it finely. Wipe the platter clean with a clean cloth dipped in very hot water.[A]
12. Spread the chopped tomato and cucumber mixture around the fish and sprinkle the chopped aspic over. Tuck a few lemon slices into the 'salad' and cover the fish eye with the stuffed olive if you wish.

[A] The fish can be left to marinate overnight in the refrigerator. Bring to room temperature an hour before cooking. The fish can also be left in its cooking liquid overnight once it has been cooked. Keep in a very cool place, but not in the refrigerator. Alternatively, finish the dish a day in advance and keep chilled, garnishing just before serving.

Whole sea bass in aspic

PRAWNS WITH TOMATO AND SHERRY SAUCE

Serves 6
1 kg (2 lb) cooked, unshelled prawns
600 ml (1 pint) water
75 g (3 oz) unsalted butter
1 large onion, peeled and finely chopped
2–3 garlic cloves, peeled and finely chopped
2 large beef tomatoes, blanched, peeled and coarsely chopped
2 tablespoons finely chopped mint leaves or 1 tablespoon dried mint
pinch of sugar (optional)
4 tablespoons dry sherry
5 tablespoons double cream
freshly ground allspice
Maldon or sea salt
freshly ground black pepper

Preparation time: 30 minutes
Cooking time: 1¼ hours

1. Shell the prawns, keeping the roes separately if wished.
2. Put the heads and shells into a large pan, cover with the water and bring to the boil, then simmer, uncovered, for 30 minutes. Strain, then return to the pan and boil hard for 4–5 minutes until reduced to about 125 ml (4 fl oz).
3. Melt the butter in another pan, add the onion and sweat for 10 minutes until nicely softened. Add the garlic, tomatoes, mint and the reduced prawn stock. Stir in the roes if you have kept them, then bring the liquid to a simmer and cook, very slowly, for about 20–30 minutes until quite thick.
4. Add a pinch of sugar if necessary to bring out the full flavour of the tomatoes, then stir in the sherry, cream, allspice, salt and lots of pepper. Add the prawns and simmer for 5 minutes to heat them through, then pile into a warmed serving dish and serve immediately.

MINT STUFFED TROUT

Serves 6
6 rainbow trout, about 275 g (10 oz) each in weight,
cleaned but heads and tails left on
16 sprigs fresh mint, leaves stripped from the stalks,
stalks reserved
100 g (4 oz) unsalted butter
Maldon or sea salt
freshly ground black pepper
3 tablespoons fresh orange juice
6 tablespoons double cream (optional)
freshly ground allspice
orange slices and mint sprigs, to garnish

Preparation time: 10–15 minutes
Cooking time: 20–30 minutes
Oven: 180°C, 350°F, Gas Mark 4

1. Rinse the trout in cold water and pat dry.
2. Chop the mint leaves finely, lightly crushing them to release some of the oils, then divide equally between the fish, stuffing them well into the cavity through which the trout were cleaned.

3. Use 25 g (1 oz) of the butter to grease 6 pieces of foil large enough to fit the fish comfortably with a good seal at the top (to make unwrapping easy), then put the mint stalks on the foil to make a bed for the fish. Place the fish on top and dot with the remaining butter cut into small pieces.
4. Sprinkle lightly with salt, generously with pepper, then dribble a little orange juice over each fish and seal the parcels.
5. Place on an ovenproof serving dish or roasting pan and cook in the preheated oven for 20–30 minutes until the fish flakes easily.
6. Transfer the parcels to a serving platter if necessary.
7. Pour the cream into a saucepan and bring quickly just to the boil. Open the tops of the parcels, drizzle a tablespoon of hot cream (if using) over each fish, then sprinkle with allspice. Garnish and serve at once with a tomato salad, crusty bread to mop up the lovely juices and a chilled Loire wine.

CLOCKWISE FROM BOTTOM: *Quenelles; Mint stuffed trout; Baked halibut with fennel and vermouth*

BAKED HALIBUT WITH FENNEL AND VERMOUTH

Serves 6
6 halibut steaks, 175–225 g (6–8 oz) each
2 large fennel bulbs, finely sliced, leaves chopped
175 g (6 oz) butter
2–3 garlic cloves, peeled and crushed
100 ml (3½ fl oz) dry Vermouth
finely ground sea salt or Maldon salt
freshly ground black pepper

Preparation time: 5 minutes
Cooking time: 30–35 minutes
Oven: 180°C, 350°F. Gas Mark 4

1. Rinse off any blood from the fish steaks and pat dry.
2. Blanch the fennel bulbs in a large pan of boiling water for 2 minutes, then drain thoroughly.
3. Melt 50 g (2 oz) of butter, add the fennel bulbs and garlic and cook gently for 10 minutes until softened.
4. Lightly grease an ovenproof serving dish, then spread the fennel, with its butter, over the base. Mash the remaining butter with the Vermouth, a little salt and a generous amount of pepper, then spread over the fish.
5. Cook in the preheated oven for 18–25 minutes until the fish just flakes easily, then serve at once, with the chopped fennel leaves sprinkled on top.

QUENELLES

Serves 6
450 g (1 lb) pike, sole, turbot or salmon fillets
4 egg whites, size 1
500 ml (18 fl oz) double cream
½ teaspoon lemon juice
finely ground sea salt
freshly ground white pepper
pinch of ground nutmeg
For the sauce:
300 ml (½ pint) milk
300 ml (½ pint) single cream
1 bay leaf
ground allspice
90 g (3½ oz) unsalted butter
3 tablespoons flour
1 small onion, peeled and minced or grated
225 g (8 oz) fresh tomatoes, blanched, skinned and chopped (or canned tomatoes, drained and chopped), seeds discarded
½ garlic clove, peeled and crushed
1 tablespoon finely chopped fresh parsley

Preparation time: 30–40 minutes, plus chilling
Cooking time: 50 minutes

1. Chop the fish, then blend to a smooth purée with the egg whites – preferably in a processor. If working by hand, mash the fish first, then mash again with the eggs, pounding very hard to obtain a smooth paste. Sieve to remove the bones.
2. Whip the cream until it holds soft peaks, then fold very thoroughly into the fish purée, until completely absorbed. (Again, if not using a food processor and working by hand, it helps to stand the bowl of fish in another bowl full of crushed ice.)
3. Stir in the lemon juice, salt, white pepper and nutmeg, then chill for at least 3 hours.[A]
4. About half an hour before serving make the sauce. Put the milk and cream in a pan with the bay leaf and a good grinding of allspice. Slowly bring to just under boiling point. Strain. In another pan, melt 50 g (2 oz) butter, stir in the flour and cook for 2 minutes. Take the pan off the heat and stir in a little of the strained milk. Mix until smooth, then return the pan to the heat and gradually add the rest of the milk, stirring between each addition. Season lightly with salt and white pepper, then simmer the béchamel gently for 20 minutes, stirring frequently.
5. Meanwhile, melt another 25 g (1 oz) butter in a separate pan, add the onion and cook gently for 5 minutes. Add the tomatoes and garlic and increase the heat. Cook until most of the tomato liquid has evaporated, but don't let them dry out completely (if they are too watery, the sauce will be too). Simmer slowly for 8–10 minutes until very soft, mashing them with a spoon every now and again to achieve a smooth purée.
6. Stir into the béchamel, little by little, mixing thoroughly and evenly, then keep warm by standing the pan over another full of simmering water. Cover with a butter paper to prevent a skin forming.[A]
7. Fill a large, wide shallow pan with water and bring barely to simmering point. Keep at the lowest possible heat, if the water is boiling the quenelles will disintegrate during cooking.
8. Using 2 dessert or tablespoons, dipped in cold water, (have a bowl of cold water by you, ready for re-dipping the spoons), shape spoonfuls of the fish mixture into nice plump ovals. Gently slide each one into the pan (do this in two batches unless you have a huge pan) and cook for 4 minutes, then carefully turn them over and poach for another 4 minutes. Remove with a slotted spoon, drain on paper towels and transfer to a plate. Keep warm by placing the plate over another pan of gently simmering water while you are cooking the rest.
9. Arrange the quenelles on individual plates, pour some sauce over each and serve immediately.

[A] The mixture may be prepared up to 24 hours in advance then covered and kept chilled. The sauce may be made up to 2 hours in advance; cover with a butter paper until needed then reheat in a bowl standing over a pan of hot water. Stir in a little more cream if it has thickened too much.

PAUPIETTES OF SOLE

Serves 8

24 small fillets of sole, bones and skins, heads and tails
reserved
Maldon or sea salt
freshly ground black pepper
1 small onion, peeled and finely sliced
few celery leaves
3 parsley sprigs
1 mace blade
6 white peppercorns, lightly crushed
300 ml (½ pint) cold water
For the herb butter:
3 anchovy fillets, chopped and pounded
175 g (6 oz) unsalted butter, softened
6 tablespoons fresh breadcrumbs
1 tablespoon Dijon mustard
3 tablespoons finely chopped fresh parsley
2 tablespoons finely chopped fresh dill
3 tablespoons finely chopped fresh tarragon
1 tablespoon lemon juice
freshly ground white pepper
For the sauce:
300 ml (½ pint) dry white wine
2 egg yolks (size 1)
5 tablespoons double cream
sprigs of fresh herbs, to garnish

Preparation time: 20–30 minutes
Cooking time: 30 minutes
Oven: 180°C, 350°F, Gas Mark 4

1. Put the fillets on a flat surface, sprinkle lightly with salt and black pepper and leave aside.
2. Put the fish trimmings into a saucepan with the onion, celery leaves, parsley, mace blade, peppercorns and water. Bring to the boil and simmer for 15 minutes.
3. Mash the anchovies into the butter, add the bread-crumbs, mustard and herbs, mixing in well. Add the lemon juice, salt and pepper, then beat until smooth.
4. Spread some of the butter over each fillet, roll them up and fix with a cocktail stick.
5. Lightly butter an ovenproof serving dish into which the rolls will fit snugly side by side.
6. Strain the stock, and mix with the wine, then pour over the paupiettes. Cover with a butter paper and cook in the preheated oven for 10 minutes, turning once.
7. Take out of the oven and pour off the cooking juices into a small pan, then keep the sole warm in the turned off oven with the door ajar.
8. Boil the liquid hard to reduce by half. Mix the egg yolks and cream together in a small jug. Stir 2 table-spoons of the reduced juices into the eggs and cream, lower the heat and add this mixture to the pan. Stir for 2–3 minutes until lightly thickened – don't let it boil or it will curdle. Pour over the fish, garnish and serve.

SALMON IN RED WINE

Serves 6

6 salmon steaks, about 25 mm (1 inch) thick
100–150 g (4–5 oz) unsalted butter
6 shallots, finely chopped
small bunch fresh parsley, finely chopped
1 garlic clove, peeled and finely chopped
6 black peppercorns, crushed
Maldon or sea salt
300 ml (½ pint) red wine
sprig of parsley, to garnish

Preparation time: 5 minutes
Cooking time: 15–20 minutes
Oven: 190°C, 375°F, Gas Mark 5

1. Rinse the salmon quickly in cold water, then pat dry.
2. Melt 50 g (2 oz) of the butter in a large flameproof dish into which the salmon will fit snugly. Add the shallots and sweat for 2 minutes, then put in the steaks and brown for 1 minute on each side over a high heat.
3. Sprinkle over the remaining ingredients, cover with a butter paper and cook in the preheated oven for 10–15 minutes until the steaks are just done.
4. Pour off the cooking juices into a small saucepan. Meanwhile, keep the salmon warm. Cut rest of the butter into small pieces and whisk into the pan, one at a time, constantly beating until each piece is absorbed. Stop when the sauce is smooth and glossy. Pour immediately over the salmon, garnish and serve.

POACHED SALMON STEAKS WITH YOGURT SAUCE

Serves 6

6 salmon steaks, about 175–225 g (6–8 oz) each
1 onion, peeled and finely sliced
1 celery stalk, finely sliced
1 bay leaf
2 sprigs fresh parsley
1 × 5 cm (2 inch) piece orange peel
12 white peppercorns, lightly crushed
300–450 ml (½–¾ pint) dry white wine
For the sauce:
¾ teaspoon cornflour
300 ml (½ pint) plain unsweetened yogurt
finely ground sea salt
½ teaspoon coriander seeds, ground
pinch of ground cinnamon
½ teaspoon dried dill
2–3 tablespoons fresh orange juice
freshly ground black pepper
1 teaspoon arrowroot (optional)
fresh herbs, to garnish

Paupiettes of sole; Salmon in red wine; poached salmon steak with yogurt sauce

Preparation time: 10 minutes, plus cooling
Cooking time: 50 minutes

1. Rinse any blood off the salmon steaks, and pat dry.
2. To make a court bouillon put the onion, celery, bay leaf, parsley, orange peel and peppercorns in a large pan. Make the wine up to 1.2 litres (2 pints) with water and pour into the pan. Simmer for 30 minutes then set aside to cool.
3. While the stock is cooling, stabilize the yogurt. Mix the cornflour with enough cold water to make a smooth paste. Whisk the yogurt until quite smooth, then beat in the cornflour mixture and a pinch of salt. Stir well, and bring to the boil, stirring slowly and constantly, always in the same direction. When just boiling, turn the heat as low as possible and simmer, uncovered (a lid would generate condensation, which will destroy the stabilization) for 10 minutes until the yogurt is thick and creamy. Take off the heat until ready to complete the sauce.
4. Arrange the fish steaks in a single layer in a large pan. Strain over the cooled stock, bring to the boil over a moderate heat, then simmer very gently for 5–6 minutes

until the salmon is opaque and firm, taking care that it doesn't overcook. Transfer the steaks to a plate, cover and keep warm by standing over a pan of simmering water.
5. Strain the bouillon again into a clean pan and boil hard to reduce to about 150 ml (¼ pint). Add the ground coriander, cinnamon, dill, 2 tablespoons orange juice and a good grinding of black pepper, then reduce the heat and stir in the yogurt. Let the sauce simmer until slightly thickened, then taste, adding more salt if necessary. If it seems a little thin, (this will depend to a certain extent on the type of yogurt used) mix the arrowroot with a teaspoon of water, and stir a little into the sauce. Continue to stir for a few minutes more, adding the remaining arrowroot paste if the sauce is still not thickening, it should be fairly light but not liquid, about the consistency of double cream. Add the rest of the orange juice.
6. Pour the sauce over or around the steaks and serve immediately.

PINK TROUT WITH PRAWNS AND HAZELNUTS

Serves 6
6 pink trout, about 350 g (12 oz) each, cleaned but
heads and tails left on
salt
1 small onion, peeled and sliced
1 carrot, sliced
1 leek, cut into rings
few celery leaves
10 black peppercorns
1 sprig fresh parsley
1 bay leaf
1 sprig fresh fennel
1 tablespoon white wine vinegar
150 ml (¼ pint) dry white wine
900 ml (1½ pints) water
lemon slices and chives, to garnish
<u>For the sauce:</u>
½ small onion, peeled and very finely chopped
50 ml (2 fl oz) white wine
3 tablespoons white wine vinegar
finely ground sea salt
freshly ground black pepper
175–225 g (6–8 oz) unsalted butter, diced and chilled
100 g (4 oz) peeled prawns, halved
25 g (1 oz) hazelnuts, finely chopped

Preparation time: 10–15 minutes, plus cooling
Cooking time: 50 minutes

1. Rinse the fish in cold water. Rub any stubborn traces of blood with a little salt, then rinse again.
2. Make up a court bouillon using the onion, carrot, leek, celery leaves, peppercorns, parsley, bay leaf, fennel, vinegar and white wine. Add the cold water and bring to the boil, then simmer for 30 minutes. Turn off the heat and leave until tepid.
3. Arrange the fish in one layer in a large pan (a roasting pan standing over 2 rings or burners will do). Pour over the strained bouillon and slowly bring to the boil, then simmer over a very low heat for 7–9 minutes, until the flesh flakes easily (test with the point of a sharp knife near the gills to avoid puncturing the skin).
4. While the fish is cooking, start the sauce. Put the onion, white wine and vinegar into a small pan. Cook until the onions are tender and the liquid has evaporated down to 2 tablespoonfuls. Remove from the heat.
5. Transfer the fish to a serving dish and keep warm while finishing the sauce – do not start the sauce before the fish are cooked because it must be cooked without interruption and served as soon as it is ready.
6. Return the pan to the heat, stir once or twice, then season with a little salt and pepper.
7. Have a bowl of very cold water (add a few ice cubes if necessary) ready by the cooker. Whisk in one piece of chilled butter, beating vigorously over a low heat. When

it has melted, whisk in another, lifting the pan off the heat between additions to prevent the sauce becoming too hot, which would make it curdle. If the sauce appears oily or looks in danger of separating at any stage, remove from the heat and immediately plunge the bottom of the pan into the cold water. Once sufficiently cooled, return to the heat and continue whisking in butter. The sauce will thicken to the consistency of a thinnish mayonnaise. Keep adding the butter, piece by piece, until creamy. Check after 175 g (6 oz) butter has been added, if the sauce is not thick enough, whisk in the rest.

8. Quickly stir in the prawns and hazelnuts and whisk for another 1–2 minutes, lift the pan off the heat for a moment or two if the sauce becomes too hot.

9. Pour the sauce over the fish, sprinkle the chives over, garnish and serve at once.

GRILLED SOLE WITH LIME BUTTER

Serves 6
6 Dover soles, 275–350 g (10–12 oz) each
175 g (6 oz) unsalted butter, softened
grated rind of 1 lime
3 tablespoons fresh lime juice
1 × 25 mm (1 inch) piece fresh root ginger, peeled and grated
finely ground sea salt or Maldon salt
freshly ground black pepper
finely chopped fresh parsley

Preparation time: 5–15 minutes
Cooking time: 10–20 minutes

1. To skin the sole start with the black skin, make a cut with a very sharp knife just above the tail. Slip the knife under the skin and loosen enough to give you a good grip (it sometimes helps to dip your fingers into salt before taking hold of the skin). Holding the tail very firmly in one hand (again salting the fingers first) pull the skin sharply away from the flesh. When you reach the head, merely snip the skin off with sharp scissors, leaving the head intact. Repeat on the other side.

2. Rinse the sole and pat dry, then arrange on a grill rack (if they do not all fit at once, cook in two batches, keeping the first batch warm).

3. Mash the butter with all the ingredients except the parsley, then spread about a tablespoon over one side of each fish.

4. Grill, butter side up, under a fairly high heat, for 3–5 minutes depending on the thickness of the fish (5 minutes per side is enough for a sole 25 mm (1 inch) thick). Turn the fish over, spread the second side of each with a tablespoon of the butter, and grill until opaque and tender. Transfer to a serving dish and pour the pan juices over. If necessary, keep warm while cooking the rest of the fish. Sprinkle with parsley and serve at once.

MONKFISH FILLETS WITH GARLIC, PINE NUTS AND PARSLEY

Serves 6
1.5 kg (3 lb) tailpiece monkfish, skinned and cleaned
finely ground sea salt
freshly ground black pepper
4 tablespoons lemon juice
4 tablespoons flour
4 tablespoons oil
50 g (2 oz) unsalted butter
2–4 garlic cloves, peeled and finely chopped
50 g (2 oz) pine nuts
6 tablespoons finely chopped fresh parsley
parsley sprigs, to garnish

Preparation time: 10 minutes
Cooking time: 20 minutes

1. To remove the bone from the monkfish, slip a thin, sharp pointed knife between the bone and the flesh, sliding it all around the bone to free it from the fish. Then push the knife out towards the edge of the piece, cutting it in half horizontally. The flesh can now be lifted, scraping it away from the bone right down to the end. Slice each 'triangular' half into 3 triangular long fillets, or cube them if you prefer.

2. Season with salt and black pepper, then sprinkle 3 tablespoons lemon juice over. Dip each fillet lightly in flour, shaking off the excess.

3. Heat the oil with the butter in a large wide shallow pan. When just about bubbling, add the fish and fry until lightly golden on both sides, then reduce the heat, add the garlic and cook for 10–15 minutes, turning the fish once, until firm and opaque.

4. Transfer to a warmed serving dish, add the pine nuts and parsley to the pan and stir for a minute. Pour the sizzling butter over the fish, sprinkle with the remaining lemon juice, garnish and serve.

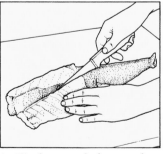

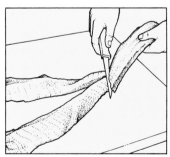

1. *Slice between the bone and flesh along the length of the fillet.*

2. *Work all round bone in this way. Lift bone and scrape off last pieces of flesh.*

Pink trout with prawns and hazelnuts;
Monkfish fillets with garlic, pine nuts and parsley

BASS BAKED WITH MANGETOUT

An exquisitely simple but delicious dish. The only requirement is a fish of the utmost freshness – look for firmness of flesh, brightness of eye, and gleaming skin with its beautiful steel grey and shiny silver markings.

Serves 6
100 g (4 oz) unsalted butter
1.5 kg (3 lb) sea bass, bream or grey mullet, cleaned, then head and tail cut off, fish boned
300 ml (½ pint) dry white wine
3–4 garlic cloves, peeled and finely chopped
½ teaspoon ground cinnamon
Maldon or sea salt
freshly ground black pepper
6 tablespoons fresh parsley, finely chopped
350 g (12 oz) mangetout
3–4 tablespoons lemon juice
lemon twists, to garnish

Preparation time: 5 minutes
Cooking time: 45 minutes
Oven: 190°C, 375°F, Gas Mark 5

1. Rub a large ovenproof serving dish with a little of the butter, then place the bass in it, leaving room on either side to add the mangetout.
2. Cut the rest of the butter into small pieces and dot all over the fish, then pour over the wine and sprinkle with the garlic, cinnamon, salt and lots of pepper, finally covering with the parsley. Lay on a butter paper and cook in the preheated oven for 40 minutes.
3. Meanwhile blanch the mangetout for 30 seconds in boiling water. Remove the butter paper, put the mangetout around the bass, spooning a little of the melted butter over them, then sprinkle both the fish and the mangetout with lemon juice and bake for another 5–6 minutes until the mangetout are just done but still crunchy and the fish flakes easily when tested with a fork. Garnish and serve at once with crusty bread.

SKATE WITH BLACK BUTTER

Skate is one of the few fish that should not be eaten immediately it is caught. Gelatinous by nature, which makes it a joy to bone, a gluey coating sticks to the fish for about 12 hours after it is out of the water. Thereafter it can be rinsed off, though the fish will still feel sticky and will smell slightly of ammonia. This however is quite normal, the smell does not mean the fish is off – but rather that it is ready for cooking – and will disappear in that process.

Serves 6
6 pieces skate wing, about 225 g (8 oz) each, preferably middle strips.
1.2 litres (2 pints) water
4 tablespoons wine vinegar
1 × 5 cm (2 inch) piece lemon rind
1 onion, peeled and sliced
12 white peppercorns, lightly crushed
1 carrot, sliced
¼ teaspoon finely ground sea salt or Maldon salt
100 g (4 oz) unsalted butter
1 tablespoon capers, chopped
3 tablespoons finely chopped fresh parsley
parsley sprig, to garnish

Preparation time: 5 minutes, plus cooling
Cooking time: 45 minutes

1. Rinse the fish in cold water.
2. Make a court bouillon with the cold water, 2 tablespoons vinegar, the lemon rind, onion, peppercorns, carrot and salt. Bring to the boil and simmer for 30 minutes, then take off the heat and allow to cool, about 30 minutes (plunging the pan into a basin of very cold water will speed up this process).
3. Put the fish in one layer in a large pan. Strain the cooled bouillon over, and slowly bring to the boil. Allow to bubble for 5 seconds, then cook over the lowest possible heat – the liquid should barely simmer – for 12–15 minutes until the fish is cooked. Transfer the fish to a hot serving dish.
4. Melt the butter in a frying pan and cook over a medium heat until a deep golden colour (despite the name the butter should not turn black – when it would be burnt). Cook for a few seconds only, then pour it over the fish.
5. Quickly pour the remaining vinegar into the pan and bring to the boil over a high heat. Stir in the capers and chopped parsley and pour over the fish immediately. Garnish with a parsley sprig and serve very hot with buttered, parsleyed new potatoes and a green salad, if wished.

Skate with black butter; Bass baked with mangetout

COLD RED MULLET IN CURRIED TOMATO SAUCE

A beautiful dish, both in colour and taste, for a hot summer's evening. To give an oriental touch, you could add a few sultanas and pine nuts to the sauce and serve on saffron rice.

Serves 6
150 ml (¼ pint) olive oil
1 large onion, finely chopped
4 large beef tomatoes, or 1 kg (2 lb) sweet fresh tomatoes, blanched, skinned and roughly chopped
3 garlic cloves, finely chopped
1–2 teaspoons curry powder
150 ml (¼ pint) fish stock (page 7)
1 teaspoon finely chopped marjoram, or ½ teaspoon dried marjoram
freshly ground allspice
Maldon or sea salt
freshly ground black pepper
6 red mullet, each about 225 g (8 oz) in weight, cleaned but left whole with livers
3–4 tablespoons lemon juice
½ teaspoon sugar
To garnish:
small bunch fresh coriander leaves, finely chopped
lemon wedges

Preparation time: 15 minutes
Cooking time: 55–60 minutes (excluding fish stock)

1. Heat 100 ml (3½ fl oz) of the oil in a large pan, add the onion and sweat gently for 10 minutes.
2. Add the tomatoes to the pan, together with the garlic, and cook for a further 5 minutes until the tomatoes begin to disintegrate.
3. Stir in the curry powder to taste, add the fish stock, marjoram, allspice, a good seasoning of salt and pepper, then simmer gently for 20–25 minutes until the sauce is quite thick with not much liquid.
4. Carefully pat the fish quite dry with paper towels. Heat the remaining oil in a large frying pan until smoking, then add the mullet. Cook for 4–5 minutes on each side over a medium heat until they are quite crisp and completely cooked.
5. Add 3 tablespoons lemon juice to the sauce, then pour over the fish, turn the heat a little lower and simmer gently for another 3–4 minutes. Take off the heat, taste the sauce adding more lemon or a little sugar if necessary. Transfer to a serving dish and leave to cool to room temperature, then chill. Garnish before serving. [A]

[A] May be prepared up to 24 hours in advance. Take out of the refrigerator 20–30 minutes before serving, so that the fish is still chilled but the flavours have had some time to 'breathe'.

LOBSTER WITH ARTICHOKE HEARTS

Serves 6
6 globe artichokes
3 cooked lobsters, about 750 g (1½ lb) each
75 g (3 oz) unsalted butter
300 ml (½ pint) dry white wine
300 ml (½ pint) crème fraîche (see page 17)
finely ground sea salt
freshly ground black pepper
pinch of ground nutmeg
3 tablespoons finely chopped fresh chervil or flat-leaved parsley
lemon wedges, to serve

Preparation time: 45 minutes–1 hour, plus cooling
Cooking time: 40–50 minutes

1. Break off the artichoke stalks. Put the heads into a large pan, cover with water and bring to the boil. Cover and cook for 30–40 minutes until a leaf pulls out easily. Drain and cool.[A]
2. Meanwhile, to prepare the lobster yourself, you will need a cleaver or large, heavy, sharp knife. Lay the lobsters with their heads away from you, shells uppermost, and halve lengthways with a good strong blow down the centre of the back. From each one remove and discard the little sac near the head (this is the stomach), pull out the thin black vein running along the body (the gut). Remove the corals (roes) if there are any, and put in a bowl.
3. Next scrape out the pale green soft meat (the tomally or liver) and add to the corals, then remove the soft pinky head meat and add that too to the bowl. The feathery gills should be taken out and discarded, but the soft flesh underneath them can be added to the corals.
4. Now extract the tail flesh and put in a separate dish. Crack the claws with a sharp blow, pull out the meat and add to the tail flesh. If you wish, you can also extract the meat from the next largest pair of legs, but these, and the shells can make an excellent soup. Scrub the shells and dry. Chop the tail meat into chunks.
5. When the artichokes are cool enough to handle, pull off all the leaves (keep them to serve cold with a vinaigrette), then scrape off all the furry 'chokes' and trim and chop the hearts.
6. Melt 50 g (2 oz) butter in a large frying pan, add the tail meat and chopped artichoke hearts, and cook for 2–3 minutes, turning until golden. Transfer with a slotted spoon to a plate and keep warm by standing over a pan of simmering water.
7. Add the wine to the pan, stir, then boil hard for 2 minutes. Reduce the heat and simmer, not too slowly, for 4–5 minutes until reduced by about half.
8. Stir in the crème fraîche, season with salt, pepper and nutmeg, stir the head meat, liver and roes into the pan. Let the sauce bubble for 3–4 minutes until slightly

thickened, then briskly whisk in the remaining butter.
9. Pile the lobster meat and artichokes into the cleaned shells, then pour the sauce over and sprinkle with chervil or parsley. Serve immediately with wedges of lemon, if wished. This is a rich dish, so a crisp green salad is the only accompaniment needed.

[A] The artichokes may be cooked up to 24 hours in advance then covered with cling film and kept chilled.

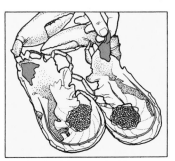 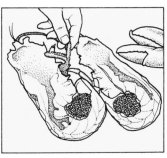

1. *Cut the lobster in half. Remove stomach sac and black vein from both halves.*

2. *Take out corals, liver and pink head meat. Remove the feathery gills, then scrape out flesh underneath.*

TRUITE AU BLEU

Serves 6
6 rainbow trout, cleaned but left whole, about 250 g (9 oz) each
Maldon or sea salt
6 tablespoons white wine vinegar
150 g (5 oz) unsalted butter
2 tablespoons creamed horseradish
1 tablespoon lemon juice
chervil and dill sprigs, to garnish

Preparation time: 2 minutes
Cooking time: 7–8 minutes

1. Rub any stubborn traces of blood on the fish with a little salt, then set aside, unrinsed.
2. Bring a large pan of water, about 2.25 litres (4 pints), to the boil, add the vinegar and a pinch of salt, then gently drop the trout into the pan. Simmer over a gentle heat for 7–8 minutes until just done.
3. Meanwhile, put the butter into a heavy-based saucepan and melt over a gentle heat. As soon as the butter starts melting, whisk, and continue to whisk all the time, so that the butter stays creamy-coloured and rather thick – as opposed to melting into a golden thin liquid.
4. Beat in the horseradish, then immediately the butter has all melted, remove the pan from the heat and whisk in the lemon juice. Pour into a warmed sauceboat.
5. Remove the fish to serving plates, garnish and serve immediately with the sauce handed round separately.

CHICKEN TURBOT
PORTUGUESE-STYLE

Serves 6
1 chicken turbot, about 1.5 kg (3–3½ lb) in weight,
cleaned but left whole
750 g (1½ lb) potatoes
2 large Spanish onions
150 ml (¼ pint) olive oil
Maldon or sea salt
freshly ground white pepper
freshly grated nutmeg
1½ tablespoons tomato purée
175 ml (6 fl oz) white wine
4 tablespoons finely chopped fresh parsley
2 sprigs fresh thyme, leaves stripped from the stalks
50 g (2 oz) black olives, stoned
lemon wedges, to garnish

Preparation time: 15 minutes
Cooking time: 1–1¼ hours
Oven: 180°C, 350°F, Gas Mark 4;
then: 190°C, 375°F, Gas Mark 5

1. Rinse the turbot in cold water, then make a thin slit along the backbone, on the knobbly-skinned side to keep it flat during cooking.
2. Slice the potatoes and Spanish onions thinly, either using a mandoline or the slicing blade of a food processor.
3. Coat the bottom of a large ovenproof serving dish, or roasting pan, with 3–4 tablespoons olive oil, swirling it around. Place the potatoes in a layer on the bottom, then cover with a layer of onions. Season with salt, pepper and lots of nutmeg, then dribble over another 3 tablespoons of the olive oil.
4. Bake in the preheated oven for 20 minutes. Remove and place the turbot on top of the onions. Lightly season with salt and pepper, then mix the tomato purée with the white wine, parsley and thyme leaves and pour all over the fish. Sprinkle with the remaining oil and bake for 20 minutes, then raise the heat and bake for a further 20–30 minutes until the fish flakes easily.
5. Scatter over the olives, garnish with the lemon wedges and serve at once.

Lobster with artichoke hearts; Truite au bleu

SCALLOPS WITH PERNOD

Scallops, like oysters, are best when there is an 'R' in the month. Frozen scallops are available now but are better kept for mousselines or to flavour sauces. In this dish freshness is of the essence and the corals – not usually frozen – add vital taste and colour.

Serves 6
18 large scallops, prepared (page 24), deep shells
scrubbed and dried
75 g (3 oz) unsalted butter
3 shallots, peeled and finely chopped
1 small garlic clove, peeled and finely chopped
2 tablespoons flour
Maldon or sea salt
freshly ground black pepper
1 tablespoon Pernod
120 ml (4 fl oz) double cream
2 tablespoons finely chopped fresh parsley
1 tablespoon lemon juice
parsley sprig, to garnish

Preparation time: 20 minutes
Cooking time: 10 minutes

1. Remove the corals and cut the white part of the scallops into 2 round discs.
2. Melt the butter in a large frying pan, add the shallots and sweat gently for 5 minutes. Add the garlic and cook for 1 minute.
3. Dip the scallop rounds into the flour, shaking off the excess, then add to the pan. Sprinkle with salt and pepper and cook for 3–4 minutes, turning once until firm and opaque.
4. Add the corals and Pernod. Let the liquid bubble for 1 minute, then remove the scallops and corals and divide between the shells.
5. Pour the cream into the pan, boil for 2 minutes to thicken the sauce slightly, stirring. Beat in the parsley and lemon juice and pour over the scallops. Garnish and serve.

Variation
You could also use a mixture of plaice fillets and scallops. Cut the fillets into small, thin strips.

HERRINGS WITH CUCUMBER AND ROE SAUCE

Cucumber is a good partner to the rich herring, and combines beautifully with the roes to make a lovely smooth sauce.

Serves 6
6 herrings with roes, cleaned, and roes reserved separately
100 g (4 oz) unsalted butter
1 small onion, peeled and finely chopped
1 small cucumber, peeled, seeded and finely diced
1 garlic clove, peeled and crushed
2 tablespoons finely chopped fresh tarragon
2 tablespoons finely chopped fresh chives
Maldon or sea salt
freshly ground white pepper
1–2 tablespoons lemon juice
300 ml (½ pint) soured cream
3 tablespoons olive oil, plus extra if necessary
flour, for dusting
lemon slices and chives (optional), to garnish
cucumber slices, to serve

Preparation time: 10 minutes
Cooking time: 20–25 minutes

1. Cut the heads and tails off the herrings, then slit in half and remove the backbone (page 43).
2. Melt 40 g (1½ oz) of the butter in a pan, add the onion, cucumber and garlic, then sweat gently for 15 minutes until soft.
3. Blend to a thick purée in a liquidizer or food processor.
4. Melt another 40 g (1½ oz) of the butter in the same pan, add the roes and cook quickly for 2 minutes, then mash thoroughly, and pour on the puréed cucumber and onion.
5. Add the chopped tarragon and chives, salt, white pepper, lemon juice and soured cream and bring to the boil, then turn the heat down and simmer while cooking the herrings.
6. Melt the remaining butter and the oil in a large frying pan. When very hot, dip the herrings into the flour, shaking off the excess and add 2, opened flat out, to the pan. Cook on each side for 1½–2 minutes until crisp and golden, then transfer to a warmed serving plate. Cook the rest quickly, adding a little more oil if necessary to the pan.
7. Pour the sauce over the fish and garnish with lemon slices and chives, if wished. Serve at once with cucumber slices.

Herrings with cucumber and roe sauce; Whiting with chicory and orange; Scallops with Pernod

WHITING WITH CHICORY AND ORANGE

Serves 6
6 whiting, filleted (see method)
1 small onion, peeled and finely sliced
1 carrot, sliced lengthways
1 celery stalk, sliced
3 parsley sprigs
5 cm (2 inch) piece lemon peel
450 ml (¾ pint) water
Maldon or sea salt
2 Seville oranges
175 g (6 oz) unsalted butter
6 large heads chicory, root ends trimmed off, the heads sliced in half lengthways
freshly ground black pepper
3 tablespoons finely chopped fresh chervil or tarragon
1 large sweet orange, finely sliced, to garnish

Preparation time: 30–40 minutes
Cooking time: about 40 minutes–1 hour
Oven: 190°C, 375°F, Gas Mark 5

1. Whiting are usually filleted through the back, so that when opened out they are kipper-shaped and in one piece. Cut off the heads and tails, then, holding the fish in a damp cloth to prevent slipping, slit all the way down the backbone, sliding the knife into the flesh as near the bone as possible. Open the fish out, turn it skin side up and press all the way down the bone. Turn them over again and slip out the bone, then clean out the innards and discard them. Rinse the fish in cold water and pat dry.
2. Put the fish heads, tails and bones into a large saucepan, add the onion, carrot, celery, parsley sprigs, lemon peel and water, then bring to the boil. Simmer for 20 minutes, adding a small pinch of salt for the last 5 minutes. Strain into a jug and squeeze in the juice of 1 Seville orange (or 1 sweet orange and half a lemon).
3. Meanwhile, place the fish on a dish and sprinkle with the juice of the second Seville orange (or 1 sweet orange and the remaining lemon), then leave aside.
4. Melt 50 g (2 oz) of the butter in a shallow pan, add the chicory, sprinkle with a little salt and pepper, then cover and sweat gently for 10–15 minutes, turning once.
5. Transfer the chicory to an ovenproof serving dish, then place the fish on top. Pour over half the strained stock and cook in the preheated oven for 15–20 minutes until the fish are just done.
6. Put the remaining stock into a small pan and boil hard until reduced to about 150 ml (¼ pint). Turn the heat down slightly, cut the rest of the butter into large pieces, and add, one at a time, whisking until absorbed into the sauce. Beat thoroughly until smooth and glossy. Taste and adjust the seasoning, then pour into a warmed sauceboat.
7. Sprinkle the fish with chervil or tarragon and garnish.

INDEX

Anchovy:
 Anchoiade 26
 Anchovy and pine nut fettucine 47
Artichoke hearts, lobster with 76
Avocado:
 Monkfish and avocado salad 58

Bacon:
 Mullet and bacon kebabs 42
 Plaice fillet and bacon salad 60
Barbecued red mullet with coriander seeds and garlic 55
Bass:
 Bass baked with mangetout 74
 Whole sea bass in aspic 66
Black bean sauce, braised cod in 37
Black butter, skate with 75
Bourride 10

Cacciucco 28
Chicket turbot Portuguese-style 77
Chicory and orange, whiting with 79
Cider baked red mullet 48
Clam chowder 14
Coconut milk, curried prawns and noodles in 31
Cod:
 Baked cod steaks with mustard seeds 50
 Braised cod in black bean sauce 37
 Cod sofrito 23
 Cod steaks in fresh coriander sauce 48
 Layered fish pie 46
 Paprika cod salad 64
 Salt cod fritters 52
Coriander sauce, cod steaks in 48
Coriander seeds and garlic, barbecued red mullet with 55
Coriander seeds, poached smoked haddock with 44
Crab:
 Crab and spinach chowder 17
 Crab sticks with sesame seed mayonnaise 9
 Dressed crab salad 59
Cucumber and roe sauce, herrings with 79
Cucumbers, marinated 12
Curried haddock fritters 28
Curried prawns and noodles in coconut milk 31

Devilled kipper tart 36
Devilled sardine paste 19

Fennel:
 Baked halibut with fennel and Vermouth 69
 Red mullet on fennel stalks with rouille 27
 Smoked haddock and fennel soup 16
Fish:
 Baked fish with pine nut sauce 35
 Bourride 10

Cacciucco 28
Fish and courgette moussaka 40
Fish plaki 27
Fish risotto 42
Hot and sour fish soup 17
Layered fish pie 46
Quenelles 69
Spicy fish balls 35
Steamed spiced fish 31
Stir-fried fillets with mushrooms 52

Grey mullet see Mullet

Haddock. See also Smoked haddock
 Curried haddock fritters 28
 Layered fish pie 46
 Walnut-stuffed haddock 44
Halibut:
 Baked halibut with fennel and Vermouth 69
 Parsleyed halibut kebabs 63
Herring:
 Fried herrings in oatmeal 53
 Herring-roe stuffed mushrooms 8
 Herrings with cucumber and roe sauce 79
 Marinated herring and new potato salad 56
Hot and sour fish soup 17

Kipper:
 Devilled kipper tart 36
 Hot kipper and mushroom salad 57
 Kipper pilau 40

Lime butter, grilled sole with 73
Lobster with artichoke hearts 76

Mackerel. See also Smoked mackerel
 Mackerel en papillote with gooseberries and nuts 64
 Turkish mackerel 32
Mangetout, bass baked with 74
Mediterranean prawn and broccoli salad 60
Mint-stuffed trout 68
Monkfish:
 Marinated monkfish grilled with herbs 45
 Monkfish and avocado salad 58
 Monkfish in chilli-basil sauce 36
 Monkfish fillets with garlic, pine nuts and parsley 73
 Monkfish kebabs with cumin and mint 63
Mullet, grey or red:
 Barbecued red mullet with coriander seeds and garlic 55
 Cider baked red mullet 48
 Cold red mullet in curried tomato sauce 75
 Grey mullet with herbs 39
 Mullet and bacon kebabs 42
 Red mullet on fennel stalks with rouille 27

Mushroom:
 Herring-roe stuffed mushrooms 8
 Hot kipper and mushroom salad 57
 Stir-fried fillets with mushrooms 52
Mussel chowder 15
Mussels à la crème 21
Mustard seeds, baked cod steaks with 50

Omelette Arnold Bennett 47
Orange and garlic mayonnaise 10
Oregano, grilled sardines with 24

Paprika cod salad 64
Parsleyed halibut kebabs 63
Paupiettes of sole 70
Pine nut:
 Anchovy and pine nut fettucine 47
 Baked fish with pine nut sauce 35
 Monkfish fillets with garlic, pine nuts and parsley 73
Plaice:
 Fried plaice with sesame seeds 50
 Gratinéed whole plaice 49
 Plaice fillet and bacon salad 60
 Soy marinated plaice 61
Prawn:
 Curried prawns and noodles in coconut milk 31
 Mediterranean prawn and broccoli salad 60
 Miniature prawn kebabs 11
 Pink trout with prawns and hazelnuts 72
 Prawn bisque 14
 Prawn and spinach pilav 23
 Prawn and spinach terrine 13
 Prawns with tomato and sherry sauce 67

Quenelles 69

Red mullet see Mullet
Red pepper sauce, smoked haddock with 41
Rice:
 Fish risotto 42
 Kipper pilau 40
 Prawn and spinach pilav 23
Rouille 27

Salmon. See also Smoked salmon
 Poached salmon steaks with yogurt sauce 70
 Salmon and almond quiche 39
 Salmon kebabs with Vermouth 63
 Salmon in red wine 70
 Two salmon terrine 21
Salt cod fritters 52
Sardine:
 Devilled sardine paste 19
 Grilled sardines with oregano 24
Sardines with cumin and garlic 32

Scallops with Pernod 78
Scallops provençale 24
Sea bass see Bass
Sesame seeds, fried plaice with 50
Shrimp butter 18
Skate with black butter 75
Smoked haddock:
 Omelette Arnold Bennett 47
 Poached smoked haddock with coriander seeds 44
 Scalloped smoked haddock mousselines 13
 Smoked haddock and fennel soup 16
 Smoked haddock with red pepper sauce 41
 Smoked haddock salad with watercress mayonnaise 56
Smoked mackerel mousse with marinated cucumbers 12
Smoked salmon mille-feuille 18
Sole:
 Fillets of sole en papillote with tarragon, wine and butter 55
 Goujons of sole with orange and garlic mayonnaise 10
 Grilled sole with lime butter 73
 Paupiettes of sole 70
 Sole fillets with soy and ginger 24
Soy marinated plaice 61
Spicy fish balls 35
Spinach:
 Crab and spinach chowder 17
 Prawn and spinach pilav 23
 Prawn and spinach terrine 13
Squid:
 Cacciucco 28
 Fried baby squid with garlic 29
 Squid in red wine 32

Tarragon, wine and butter, fillets of sole en papillote with 55
Trout:
 Grilled rainbow trout with ground almond paste 55
 Mint-stuffed trout 68
 Pink trout with prawns and hazelnuts 72
 Truite au bleu 76
Tuna and caper soufflé 51
Tuna creams on Chinese leaves 20
Turbot:
 Chicket turbot Portuguese-style 77
Turkish mackerel 32
Two salmon terrine 21

Walnut-stuffed haddock 44
Watercress mayonnaise 56
Whitebait:
 Fried whitebait 8
Whiting with chicory and orange 79

Yogurt sauce, poached salmon steaks with 70